MODEL RAILROADING WITH LGB

BY ROBERT SCHLEICHER

EDITED BY CARTER COLWELL

WITH THE ASSISTANCE OF
MARCY DAMON AND LINDA F. GREENBERG

Drawings by Donna W. Price

Photographs not credited were taken by Robert Schleicher

A Greenberg Publication

Copyright © 1989

Greenberg Books
Division of Kalmbach Publishing Co.
21027 Crossroads Circle
Waukesha, WI 53187
(414) 796-8776

First Edition
Second Printing

Manufactured in the United States of America

Greenberg Books, a division of Kalmbach Publishing Co., publishes the world's largest selection of Lionel, American Flyer, LGB, Marx, Ives and other toy train publications as well as a selection of books on model railroading and other collectible toys. For a complete listing of current Greenberg publications, please call 1-800-533-6644 or write to: Kalmbach Publishing Co., 21027 Crossroads Circle, Waukesha, WI 53187.

Greenberg Shows, Inc., sponsors Greenberg's Great Train, Dollhouse and Toy Shows, the world's largest of its kind. The shows feature extravagant operating train layouts, and a display of magnificent dollhouses. The shows also present a huge marketplace of model and toy trains for HO, N, and Z Scales; Lionel O and Standard Gauges; and S and 1 Gauges; plus layout accessories and railroadiana. They also offer a large selection of dollhouse miniatures and building materials, and collectible toys. Shows are scheduled each year from Massachusetts to Florida. For a list of current shows, please call (410) 795-7673 or write to Greenberg Shows, Inc., 7566 Main Street, Sykesville, MD 21784 and request a show brochure.

Greenberg Auctions, a division of Greenberg Shows, Inc., offers nationally advertised auctions of toy trains and toys. Please contact our auction manager at (410) 795-7447 for further information.

ISBN: 0-89778-089-2

Library of Congress Cataloging-in-Publication Data

Schleicher, Robert H.
    Model railroading with LGB / by Robert Schleicher ; edited by Carter Colwell ; with the assistance of Marcy Damon and Linda F. Greenberg ; photographs by Robert Schleicher ... [et al.].
        p. cm
        Bibliography: p.
        ISBN 0-89778-089-2 :
        1. Railroads — Models. 2. Ernst Paul Lehmann (Firm) I. Colwell, C. Carter. II. Damon, Marcy. III. Greenberg, Linda F. IV. Title.
    TF197. S345   1989
    625. 1'9—dc19   89-1825
                                                         CIP

Acknowledgments

LGB trains and equipment have become exceedingly popular in the last ten years. Their attractiveness, durability, and adaptability to a range of weather conditions have created myriad possibilities for their use indoors or outside.

What has been missing is an American guide to building LGB layouts. **Bob Schleicher**, an inveterate railroad writer, recognized the need for a book on model railroading with LGB and has written a practical, how-to-build-it, easy to follow guide to help hobbyists. His commitment and enthusiasm made this book possible.

Schleicher is the author of numerous books on model railroading. He also photographed most of the LGB displays shown here.

In addition, able assistance was given by **Carter Colwell**, editor of *Greenberg's Guide to LGB Trains*, first edition, and an avid LGB collector and layout builder (both inside and out). And, the advice of "fine-tuners" **James Strong**, **Fred Shultz**, and **Michael Albertson**, members of the Washington-Virginia-Maryland Garden Layout Club, was exceedingly helpful. The Club is very well known for its impressive LGB displays. **Larry Lyons** of Sails and Rails, a shop filled with LGB, in Savannah, Georgia, reviewed the manuscript and made a number of very useful suggestions.

In Sykesville, **Marcy Damon** very capably edited, organized, and brought to fruition this long-awaited book. **Donna Price**, with G Scale Template in hand, drew all the track and wiring diagrams based on Colwell's rough sketches and helped arrange each page. **Dallas Mallerich** aided in proof-reading the technical material. **Barbara Morey** typed in much of the text. **Maury Feinstein** prepared the artwork for final publication. **Samuel Baum** assisted in the book's design and format and with **Maureen Crum** designed the cover.

Linda Greenberg
Publisher
May 1989

Robert Schleicher

Bob Schleicher is one of the fortunate few; he has combined his hobby interests with his professional abilities to become a successful, full-time writer. Bob became a hobbyist gradually. During the Second World War, when there were few toys available, he was delighted to find cardboard kits which he quickly learned how to assemble. These gave him great satisfaction. Then, in 1946, when real trains became available again, he built a Lionel layout. In 1948 he built an HO layout and in the 1950s he moved on to slot car racing.

In 1963 Bob began a part-time career in writing about the hobbies he knew so well, and this became a full-time occupation in 1966. As a writer, he has been an editor, author, and photographer as well, with books and articles on such diverse subjects as racing motorcycles, skateboards, dollhouses, radio control cars, and, of course, model railroads. He has authored *The Lionel Train Book*, *HO Model Railroading Handbook*, *Model Railroading Handbook*, Volumes I, II, and III, and *N Scale Model Railroading Manual*.

Carter Colwell

Carter Colwell likes devising ingenious layouts. Consider: after his work with Robert Schleicher, he began uprooting an indoor, around-the-wall layout, and moving it outdoors. He moved dirt, built walls, and laid track on several levels so that the lower loop-to-wye circuit interchanges with a cog railway running up the face of a rock retaining wall, which in turn joins an upper level line that spirals and loops over itself à la Rhaetian railway, and then proceeds through the garden wall to the carport at waist level.

When not playing with LGB, Colwell earns his living as a teacher at Florida's Stetson University. He is the editor of John Ottley's *Greenberg's Guide to LGB Trains*, first edition, and member #002 of the LGB Model Railroad Club. Colwell urges all LGB collectors and modelers alike to join the club's membership with him.

Table of Contents

Chapter 1
Large Scale Trains

Massive! These models are much larger, more substantial, and heftier than mere toys. In the electric-powered locomotives and rolling stock made by Ernst Paul Lehmann in Nurnberg, West Germany, an entirely new form of model railroading has been created. The factory calls the models Lehmann Gross Bahn, which translates loosely as Lehmann Large Railroad. Their logo, and popular name, is LGB.

The models are indeed large. Reasonably accurate replicas of real railroad equipment, the models are 1/22.5th the size of the real thing, made to a scale ratio of 1:22.5. HO scale models, on the other hand, are 1:87 scale, but the fourfold difference between 22.5 and 87 does not give a true picture of the bulk and heft of the LGB models. They are four times longer, four times taller, and four times wider than HO scale *narrow gauge* * equipment. That cubic difference is what makes LGB seem so large: it has 64 times the mass of comparable HO equipment.

THE BIGGEST OF THE SMALL

The charming paradox of LGB is that these huge models reproduce what in real life are tiny trains. LGB models are replicas of locomotives and rolling stock that operate on meter *gauge* track (3' 3-3/8" between the rails). American and European *standard gauge* is 4' 8-1/2" between the rails. Since the distance between the rails of LGB's *prototype* trains is narrower than standard gauge, they are called narrow gauge. The most common narrow gauge used in America was 3 feet between the rails.

The majority of the narrow gauge railroads were built before the turn of the century. It was less expensive to build smaller bridges, and bore smaller tunnels, and use tighter curves, all possible with

*All new terms, when they are first used, will be in italics; definitions may be found in the glossary at the end of the book.

This Howe truss, typical of American narrow gauge bridges and their light load capacity, is a Kenosha Railway Supply model with real nuts and bolts, tightened to keep it straight.

The narrow gauge equipment on the real Rio Grande (left) was about three-fourths the size of the standard gauge equipment. Photo from the collection of H. K. Vollrath.

narrow gauge, than to build a railroad with the larger proportions of standard gauge. Most of the narrow gauge railroads were rebuilt between 1900-1920 with broader curves, wider and sturdier bridges, and larger tunnels. Today in Europe some narrow gauge lines such as the large Rhaetian network in alpine southeastern Switzerland or the river valley feeder lines of Austria still carry payloads. Many rail lines in America are preserved in tourist lines like the one out of Durango, Colorado. There were, and still are, a number of industrial railroads and mountain lines that are narrow gauge.

From the proportions of the track gauges, 36 versus 55-1/2 inches, you might expect a narrow gauge locomotive to be about two-thirds the size of a standard gauge locomotive. In reality, narrow gauge locomotives and rolling stock are larger than that. Much of the charm of narrow gauge equipment derives from their slightly oversized bodies: the narrow gauge cars and locomotives hang over the track and over the trucks or wheels farther than similar standard gauge equipment. An experienced train watcher can usually spot at a glance narrow gauge stock, on site or in a photograph. Thus, even the prototypes of LGB are the biggest of the smallest. The LGB models retain this hefty width, which appears over-sized as compared to the track gauge.

Newer LGB models replicate American as well as European prototypes (described in Chapters 11 and 12). The meter-gauge scale of the LGB model track is close enough to the 3 foot-gauge scale of American prototypes to seem natural. In addition to those models, several of the LGB four-wheeled cars and 0-4-0T and 0-6-0T locomotives are very similar to industrial cars used in America; the little LGB KOF diesel resembles a tiny American standard gauge Plymouth switcher. The European prototype models, too, can look at home on an American-based model railroad (see modeler Robert Treat's railroad in Chapter 2).

INDOORS OR OUT?

Of all the popular toy trains available, LGB trains are the only ones designed specifically to be operated either indoors or outdoors.

INDOORS:

Indoors, the trees and other shrubbery surrounding the trains are also scale models. The plants don't live; the lighting is artificial; but it neither rains nor freezes, and the scale is uniform — even the leaves can be more or less proportional to the size of the trains. Some modelers build their *layouts* on the floor and add scenery. (See page 71.) Most indoor

So far, the mountains for Norm Grant's railroad are mere piles of dirt and weeds; they will be covered with rocks and plants in time.

LGB layouts are simply arranged around a Christmas tree or on the floor of the den or, perhaps, on a piece of indoor/outdoor carpeting; others layouts are portable, having no permanent site (see Chapter 14).

Some are built on shelves or on large, specially constructed tables. Open framework, covered with scenery, can provide special tables or shelves that raise LGB layouts nearer eye level (Chapter 8). Malcolm Furlow's mountainous layout has been featured in LGB publications since its first appearance in *Model Railroader* (Oct/Nov 86); Joe Crea's shelf-style layout has appeared there, as well as in *Railroad Model Craftsman* (Mar 85) and *Narrow Gauge and Shortline Gazette* (Sept/Oct 85). But the majority of LGB modelers seem to prefer either to build an outdoor or garden railroad or to use temporary track setups on the floor.

It is certainly possible to build an LGB layout on a table top, but for continuous running you will need at least a 5 x 9-foot table. The basic oval shown in Chapter 4 is too wide for a 4 x 8-foot board, and the double track oval is too wide for even a 5 x 9-foot ping-pong table. Both Malcolm Furlow and Joe Crea built their layouts on shelves around the walls of the room. This allows room for a narrow table so they can reach the trains to rerail them, operate couplers, or perform maintenance tasks. Other people prefer expansive table top structures, perhaps 8 x 16-feet, and built of sturdy plywood, where they can construct a mighty railroad empire.

OUTDOORS:

If you choose an outdoor layout with realistic scenery for your LGB trains, just set them up near some of the smaller bushes or flower plants in the garden. The trains are certainly realistic and the plants are not simply lifelike, but life itself. There is real dirt, real rocks, real sunlight, and real plants.

Photographs do not convey the feeling of realism obtained when operating outdoors. In the beauty of a natural setting, you do not notice that real plants' leaves are too large for the scale of the trains. You accept the plant leaves for plant leaves and the train assumes its own identity. Your eyes and mind simply do not have to make the adjustment for scale that they do on even the most perfectly scenicked indoor layout: that's a real train running through a real world.

The bright colors of the LGB trains lend another dimension to a garden. They appear to be almost a form of living flower, with their life derived not from cell structure, but from movement.

LGB trains appeal to a wide range of model railroading styles. Some people get involved in LGB trains because they like real trains. They want their LGB models to look as much like the real thing as possible. The real thing, when it comes to a steam locomotive working on a narrow gauge railroad, usually means (or meant, when steam locomotives did pull freight trains) a fairly dirty locomotive and even dirtier rolling stock. The atmosphere, similar to that recreated by modelers Robert Treat and Herb Chaudiere (see Chapter 2), reeks of coal smoke gritty with cinders. If you like realistic weathering, then paint, decals or dry transfers, and washes of chalks will make cars and locomotives look as authentically dirty as you like (see Chapter 12). Others are caught by the bright freshness of LGB's colorful cars, sparkling and clean as a nostalgic dream. This is the garden ambience created by modelers Pete Thorp and Gary Nelson. (See "Garden Railway or Outdoor Railroading?" in Chapter 2.)

STAND-OFF SCALE

The LGB equipment has details as fine as the better HO scale model railroad equipment, with crisp rivets and sharply defined braces, steam locomotive backhead gauges, and working door handles. These models rely on correct proportions, good detail, and sheer bigness to convey the feeling of realism.

If you view an LGB model railroad from three feet or more, the rolling stock look like completely accurate replicas. A number of experienced LGB model railroaders have expressed the opinion that these large scale trains are at their best when viewed from such a distance. That distance allows you to perceive the fine lettering and detailing on the models without

Part of the reverse loop on the David Charles' family layout travels across one end of the swimming pool deck.

missing the really small details like brake rigging beneath the cars, or without noticing that the *grab-irons* on the boxcars are molded on. Some cars now come with separate grab-irons, and a few have simple brake details. The large size of LGB models allows you to add even more detail, enough to make them a match for the $1000 all-brass imported models in HO or O scale. But you might be defeating the purpose of these trains if you did; they would no longer be as rugged as they are out-of-the-box, and when they hit the floor or ground, the 64-fold difference in mass could play havoc with extra detail. As it is, LGB cars have been dropped as much as six feet onto tile floors without sustaining any damage beyond temporary disassembly — the roof pops off. (But test-dropping is not recommended, especially with engines.)

RELIABLE OPERATION

LGB equipment is designed to be as sturdy as it looks. The track and locomotives are designed to be operated indoors or outdoors with 18 volts of direct or DC current (see Chapter 9). Although the main *power pack* with its 120-volt house current should be kept indoors, LGB offers a separate *throttle* (the 5012/1 speed control and reversing *switch*) that can be mounted outdoors. Since all 120-volt units are kept indoors, trains can operate in any weather as long as water or moisture is not allowed to get into the throttle itself. LGB trains can be operated in the snow and in the rain.

The trains themselves weather nicely, although engines in particular will last longer if not stored permanently outside. The cars have very few exposed metal parts, and their high grade plastic is very durable. It is wise to bring the locomotives and rolling stock indoors when the railroad is not in use, to reduce the ravages of strong sun and the infiltration of fine dust into the moving parts. Some buildings (see Chapter 11) are vulnerable to sun; most invite insect habitation, and will store more satisfactorily indoors.

The LGB track is extremely tough, with strong rail, metal joiners, and plastic clips for more secure joining. It can stay outdoors all year in just about any climate. The track will simply take on a more realistic appearance as it is exposed to the elements. An occasional cleaning of oxides from the rail top, with electrical contact cleaning fluid (but never with coarse sandpaper or other scratchy abrasive) should keep the current flowing from rail to engine wheel (see Chapter 9).

YOU, THE RAILROAD SURVEYOR

LGB model layouts share yet another quality with the real railroads and with all other scales and sizes of model railroads: they do not easily travel up hills. Track must be level and flat. Relatively gentle up and down *grades*, up to about 4 inches of climb in 100 inches of distance, are acceptable, but steeper grades can cause problems and frustration. Each of the joints between the track sections must be in nearly

A 2028D Mogul pulls modified LGB passenger cars over Norm Grant's granite fill and pine cribbing. Notice that all details are clearly visible.

perfect alignment — dips and humps at the joints are sure causes of derailments and stalled locomotives.

And once your LGB track work ventures off slabs of concrete and into the earthen world of lawn and garden, you need to prepare some special roadbed to support the track to keep it in alignment and to allow water to drain or flow, to avoid frost heaves and buckling of the roadbed and track, and to limit the growth of weeds. (See Chapters 6 and 7.) It is possible to lay an oval or even a complex layout on perfectly level grass for an afternoon's operation, but a permanent *right of way* for your railroad will need much the same preparation (as in *cuts*, *fills*, and bridges) as supplied by a real railroad's surveyor and engineer for a full-sized roadbed.

REAL RAILROAD OPERATIONS

There are dozens of specfic track plans in the various LGB books, but most of them are designed to appeal to the European enthusiast. The plans you see in this book are based on sixty years of development in the American model railroading hobby. The oval shapes may make them look like toy train plans, but the arrangement of *turnouts* provides for train routings like those of real railroads.

The track plans in Chapters 4 and 5 will give you an example of what you can do with LGB models in the least possible space. Each of those track plans may be enlarged by simply adding pairs of straight track sections at parallel joints (see Chapter 3). The outdoor layouts in Chapter 2 are examples of what is, so far, the ultimate in outdoor LGB layout construction in America. The plans and photos suggest the possibilities for operations of two or more trains over a variety of routings, through a range of scenic effects: tunnels, cuts, fills, and bridges.

What is not obvious, from the plans and photos, is precisely how the trains are operated. There are many train movement patterns, some based purely on fun and others based on how the real railroads operate. Basic optional train routings built into the track plan can make main line operations more interesting (see Chapters 4 and 5). Switching moves on an LGB layout can duplicate the actions of a small freight yard or the spotting and pickup of individual cars at industrial sidings (see Chapter 10); some modelers replace the LGB hook-and-loop couplers with operating knuckle couplers, which look more realistic, from LGB (2019/2), Delton, or Kadee (see Chapter 10). Lehmann now offers its own easily installed knuckle couplers.

The typical European model railroad enthusiast seems to enjoy complex track layouts with dozens of

Norm Grant elevated the right of way on the David Charles' layout about a foot above the earth on this granite chip fill.

switches to provide alternate train routings. Basically a spectator, he focuses on automatic routing, stopping, and starting of the trains; the turnouts are thrown automatically so the operator can rely on the train to follow its route, and simply sit back and watch the trains pick their prescribed routes through a maze of track work. Often, track side signals, used to indicate which routes are open to oncoming trains, are also operated automatically.

Many American model railroaders seem to prefer somewhat simpler track layouts. Americans often use walk-around throttles or speed controls on 12- to 20-foot long electrical cables, so they can walk beside their train as it moves around the basement or the garden. They imagine themselves to be engineers with their focus on the train itself. If a second train is operated, it is either set on an automatic control of its own, using a separate power pack, or a second operator runs that train independently. If you prefer the action of multiple train routings and imagining yourself a dispatcher, then block control and alternate routings may be your choice. (See "Engineer, Dispatcher, or Spectator?" Chapter 5.)

For further layout information, with many useful ideas from the European perspective, check the Lehmann publication *Layouts and Technical Information* (0028E). There is also an LGB model Railroad Club in America. Its 40-page illustrated newsletter is called *Big Train Operator*, and includes tips on maintenance, construction, and operations. *Garden Railways* magazine, a bimonthly publication averaging about 40 pages per issue with some color photos, emphasizes outdoor models; but the articles on locomotives, cars, and structures are applicable to indoor layouts as well. The editor, Marc Horovitz, has been extremely helpful in the preparation of this book, providing sources and background information. (See the Appendix for Clubs, Publications, and Supply Sources.)

LGB is both old and new. It is old in the prototypes of most of its equipment, the narrow gauge mites that overcame mountains. As a toy train, it continues a tradition as old as trains themselves. It is new in its glorious size — an HO modeler visiting an LGB layout commented, as he held an 0-6-2T, "It's nice to hold a locomotive big enough to cradle in your arm!" And Lehmann constantly refines its technology to increase durability, reliability, and operating possibilities.

Chapter 2
Layout Tours

The real railroads that were built with narrow gauge track were characterized by track work with tight curves, and lots of them. The locomotives were small, the rolling stock compact, and the trains often short. All of these things make it easier to squeeze a large amount of model railroad into a very small space while maintaining some degree of credibility and realism.

The smallest LGB curves are tight enough to fit a layout with continuous running (circle, oval, figure eight, etc.) onto a ping-pong table. The track plans in Chapter 3 will allow you to explore, visually, how much layout you can build into a cramped space. The layouts in this chapter are the other end of the LGB layout spectrum: model railroads that occupy the expanses of entire backyards or a full basement. This is truly large scale model railroading at its grandest. You should understand that none of the outdoor layouts were built by drawing a track plan. The curves were located and marked with a string compass in any areas in which the large radius 1600 curved track sections were NOT used. The 1600 has the minimum radius (about 46-1/2 inches) used on these outdoor layouts; most of the curves are 48- to 96-inch radius. Generally, the larger radius curves allow the models to look much more like the real thing. The tighter radius LGB curved track sections (1100, 1500) look a bit toy-like in vast outdoor settings, where there may be no apparent reason for a tight curve; but they can be useful in a *reversing loop* around the trunk of a tree in one corner of the yard.

You certainly do not need an entire backyard to enjoy model railroading with LGB equipment. The LGB track does, however, make it relatively easy to create vast empires. In this chapter, six actual layouts will be discussed. The techniques for preparing the roadbed for outdoor layouts are presented in Chapter 6 with basic landscaping techniques explained in Chapter 7.

ONE MODELER'S BASEMENT EMPIRE

The most common site for LGB layouts is NOT the backyard. Most modelers simply lay the track on the floor of a spare room, den, patio, pool deck, or basement. Most of those sites are places where the track must eventually be removed to make space for other household activities. In one particular house, however, there is a full basement, occupied originally by a furnace and a small storage room. Now the basement is the site of one of the largest and most interesting private home layouts in America.

Grade Steepness

Grade steepness may be given as a ratio or a percentage. Most LGB trains will not operate comfortably at a grade much steeper than 4 percent, which is 4 inches, (or feet, or meters) of vertical rise in 100 inches (or feet, or meters) of horizontal travel. Grade radically affects how many cars an engine can pull, although this is less true for models than for real railroads. For long trains, grades of 2 percent or less are recommended. However, weights may be added to the engine for more pulling power on grades.

A "one-in-four" or "1:4" grade rises one vertical foot in four feet of horizontal travel. Only a cog locomotive, like LGB's 2045, with rack rail, can climb this very steep grade. A one-in-four grade is the same as a 25 percent grade.

Most of a 30- x 40-foot area is filled with the layout. The original trackage was laid flat on the floor. (A diagram of the original layout is on the master control panel shown in Figure 2-1.) Next, a

This basement layout began with just the track on the floor. Adding the track up and around this mountain was next.

The basement layout was later extended up into the Hydrocal plaster mountains (see Chapter 8).

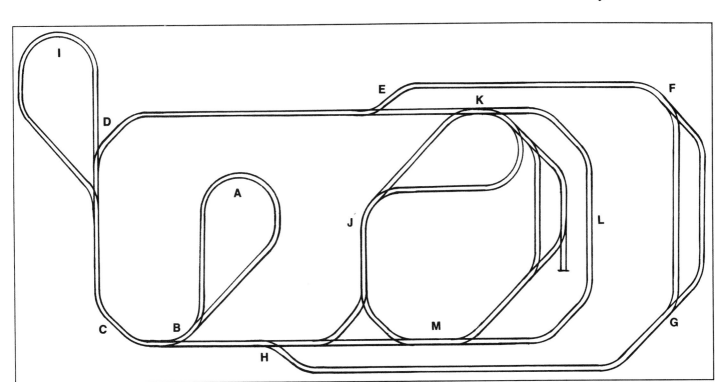

Figure 2-1: A schematic diagram of the basement layout. A through I is the longest loop-to-loop route; J to M is a separate oval route.

series of s-curves was built up and down the distant mountain. The latest extensions include a line winding up into the range of plaster mountains to a reversing loop; there is another reversing loop on the floor beneath the mountain range.

The plan was designed in place, using many boxes of LGB sectional track. After the track, with its five-foot diameter curves (1500) and large switches (1226, 1236), was in place on the floor, it was elevated on one-by-four vertical risers. The risers are spaced equal distances apart, so the risers can be cut to length with equal increments for easier carpentry and still maintain a steady grade (by spacing them equally). A spacing was selected that gave the right grade with a 1/2-inch difference in the height of each riser. For a grade a little less than 4 percent, a rise of 1/2 inch about every 14 inches is needed. (1/2 inch of rise per 12-1/2 inches of length is 4 percent.) The risers were then precut to length in 1/2-inch increments, starting with a 1/2 inch riser, then 1 inch, 1-1/2 inches, 2 inches, 2-1/2 inches, and so forth until the maximum desired elevation was reached. Instead of measuring riser spacing with a ruler or tape, one riser was located between every 13 ties. There are 11 ties in a one-foot 1100 straight (track), 14 in a 15-inch 1500 curve (track). The slight variation in tie-spacing at each LGB track section joint has no practical consequence.

The edges of the ties were then marked on sheets of 1/2 inch plywood to make a roadbed support for the track. The risers were attached to the plywood with screws and the track nailed to the plywood; a horizontal crossbar at the floor stabilizes each riser.

The 1/2 inch rise per 13 ties works out to be close to 4 percent, the practical maximum for the LGB American prototype Mogul locomotive. At least two feet of track were adjusted to be level at the top of any grade before heading the track back down. This lessens humps in the track at the beginning or end of a grade; such humps, or (at the bottom) troughs, can cause accidental uncoupling or derailments.

The layout is operated entirely by remote control; all the turnouts on the reversing loops are actuated automatically with LGB's EPL switch drive units on the turnouts, using LGB track contacts triggered by LGB magnets. The 1701 magnets are mounted on the pilots (rather than at locomotive center) so the 1700 track contacts will be activated in time to throw the turnout before the locomotive wheels reach it. A second magnet is mounted on the tender trucks so the turnout is set correctly when the locomotive is backing up. In many applications, of course, it is possible to locate the track contacts far enough ahead of the switch so that special mounting of the magnet is not necessary, and one magnet is adequate. All of the turnouts can also be operated by remote-control toggle switches on the control panel.

Each of the locomotives is fitted with the receiver for the Keller brand Onboard *carrier/command-control system* described in Chapter 9. The tethered key

One corner of Norm Grant's huge back yard layout.

pad throttle controls are long enough so an "engineer" can walk about 20 feet away from the control panel to watch the trains. The system minimizes the amount of extra wiring needed but it is still wise to run some extra jumper wires to supplement the rail joiners as they conduct current around the layout — a good precaution on a layout of this size.

The mountains are supported by vertical two-by-two boards, braced with one-by-two lumber. Plaster-soaked newspapers were draped over the vertical two-by-twos, whose tops are the peaks of the mountains. A few more supports were added to make ridges in the mountain shapes, and more tunnels were created (by techniques described in Chapter 7). Eventually, most of the background areas will be filled with mountains, leaving deep canyons to the floor as access aisles.

NORM GRANT'S
COLORADO & SOUTHERN

The spectacular wooden trestles and wooden Howe *truss bridges* shown in this book are the highlights of Norm Grant's outdoor layout. The bridges (see Color Plates), products of Kenosha Railway Supply, make Norm's layout truly unique.

The railroad meanders around a slightly hilly 50- x 100-foot backyard. The area was not leveled or seeded with grass when Norm started, so he contracted to have a few more tons of dirt dumped here and there to make mountains. The level valley floors were laboriously hand-shoveled. He used surveyor's stakes, string, and a long level to lay out the right of way and to guide him in leveling the roadbed.

The maximum grade has been held to 2 percent (2 inches rise per 100 linear inches of track). Norm finds that the LGB Moguls will pull about seven cars up that grade compared to 10 to 14 cars on the level stretches of track. A compass was made of string to swing the radii for the curves; the minimum radius is about 60 inches.

About Filler

"Filler" is a generic term for one of the sub-base sand and clay mixes used beneath driveways. This is the type of sand that actually compacts and hardens slightly (like sandstone) after it is soaked with water, by rainfall or sprinkler. It holds the track tightly enough so that no nails are needed to keep the track in place, but it is still soft enough so the track can be lifted and reused. The material can be broken up with a shovel or hoe. In the midwestern part of the country, the mix is known as "squeegee."

Most of the track work is LGB's 1.5-meter long flexible track (1000/3, 1000/5) with the long turouts (1605N, 1615N). After the roadbed is meticulously leveled, Norm positions the track and pours on the sand/clay compound. There are no wash out problems from driving rains, since he is careful to provide

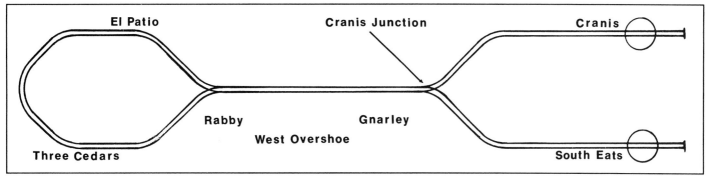

Figure 2-2: Schematic diagram of Herb Chaudiere's garden railway.

some sort of bridge over every low spot that might present potential flooding problems.

The rock work is mostly for scenic effects; he has purchased several tons of granite and other rocks from local quarries and mines. He carefully sorts out what he calls "seasoned" rocks, those that have been exposed to the air and have moss and other weathering. The "raw" rock is used for mountains and fills, the seasoned rock to simulate natural boulders along the right of way.

Norm checks the *rail joiners* for tightness once a month, but the flexible track allows for fewer joints, one about every five feet (1.5 meters). All of the turnouts are controlled with hand levers, limited production items sold by various firms that advertise in *Garden Railways* magazine. At present, a single Aristo number 5 *power pack* with a 5 amp rating is used to control the locomotives. Only two wires connect to the track, although he does plan to install a few additional pairs of wires directly to the farthest points on the track, still under construction.

Most of the foliage consists of natural small bushes and weeds that he has kept for their value in providing smaller leaf patterns. Hundreds of small trees and bushes have also been planted and more

are on the way. He uses purple (herb) sage, woolly (creeping) thyme, phlox, and mint to simulate deciduous trees; and tiny Douglas firs, Scotch pines, and junipers as coniferous plants.

HERB CHAUDIERE'S CRANIS GARDEN RAILWAY

Herb Chaudiere's LGB layout is an example of nearly all the techniques used by experienced model railroaders, but applied here to an outdoor railroad. Herb does it all the way a craftsman would, from using individually cut redwood ties and smaller rail, to operating the system on a timetable. Since there are 576 feet of actual main line track in Herb's layout, plus another 157 feet of sidings, this is quite an undertaking. It is not just LGB in operation outdoors; it is scale model railroading using LGB locomotives and cars (all with the wheel flanges reduced in size) on track hand-laid to scale model standards.

Herb builds his own structures and selects people from plastic automobile and military kits that are 1/24 scale. It is easier to work in that size because you can use the 1/2-inch-to-the-foot scale rulers designed for architects and draftsmen. There is also a wide variety of plastic cars and military accessories available for detailing scenes, probably more than in the popular model railroad O scale (1/48 scale). MPC, now a division of Ertl, has offered a 1/24 scale replica of the Civil War era General 4-4-0 locomotive that can provide useful parts for altering any LGB locomotive. Herb used their smoke box number plate for his 2-6-0, with other detail parts from Trackside Details.

Because 3/8-inch scale standard gauge has about the same gauge as LGB tracks, Herb uses the National Model Railroad Association Standards S-3 and S-4 as revised July 1986 for 3/8-inch scale, except for the tire (wheel) width and flange depth, where he uses the dimensions for 1/2-inch scale. If you are interested in creating more accurate and finer scale track work, the NMRA Standards are

Rail Measurement

Full-sized rail is measured by weight, but model rail is measured by height in thousandths of an inch. LGB is .337 inches high (the rail alone, without ties), and by conventional hobby nomenclature, would be called "code 337" rail. Rail sizes vary according to railroad and use, but standard LGB rail is much larger than scale-sized rail. Herb uses code 155, code 172, and code 190 rail to closely approximate scale rail. However, the over-sized flanges of Lehmann wheels will not operate on this smaller rail so Herb reduces the size of the wheel flanges accordingly. (Older LGB has larger flanges than the equipment made since 1978/79, and will not run on some smaller rail that the newer wheels can negotiate.)

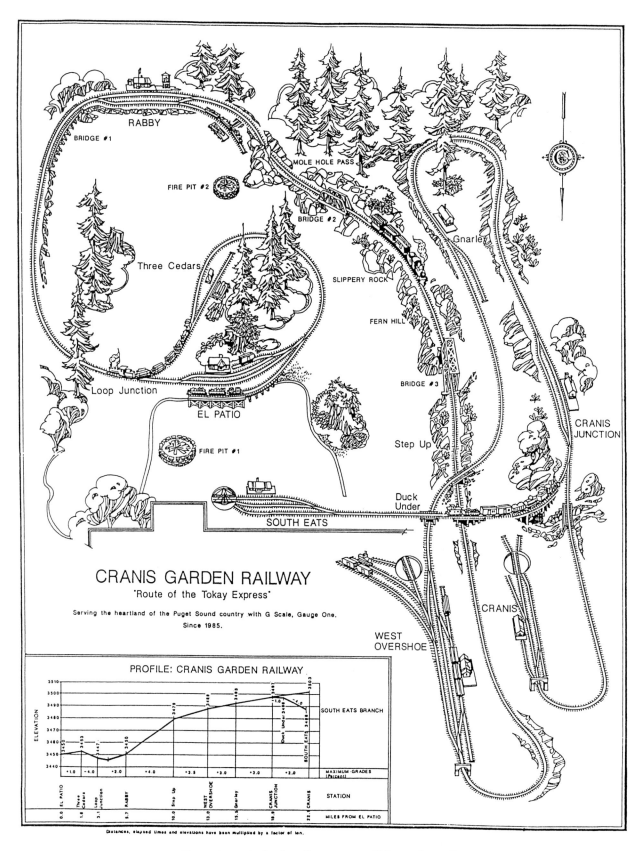

Figure 2-3: Herb Chaudiere's map of his garden railway.

invaluable; they are included with a one-year membership (see Appendix: Clubs).

He repaints each car and locomotive and applies dry transfer lettering from a drafting supply store. The cars are weathered with an airbrush. (The dry transfer lettering process and weathering techniques are described in Chapter 12.)

Because they are closer to 1/24 scale narrow gauge coupler size than most others, Herb uses O scale "tinplate" couplers (like those sold by Walthers as number 941-796). The couplers are mounted to the bodies of the cars, for greater realism. Uncoupling is accomplished manually, by simply lifting one end of the car about 1/4 inch and dropping it back on the rails.

The locomotives are operated with a command/carrier-control system. A steady 18 volts is carried in the rails; the speed and direction are adjusted by receivers in each locomotive according to signals sent through the rails. Herb also has a radio control throttle so he does not need to have a tethered throttle; he can walk along beside any train anywhere on the huge 88 x 102 foot layout. He made his own system, but Keller's Onboard control system has a radio control throttle available.

The track plan consists of four major terminals: one inside a reversing loop, one as a junction between two lines, and the other two at the ends of each of those two lines. (See Figures 2-2 and 2-3.) The last two terminals are located inside the garage and beside the back of the house. The junction terminal is also inside the garage on a second shelf directly above another terminal — the track leaves the garage's lower shelf, makes a loop out in the yard, then re-enters the garage on a shelf a foot higher than the first. The track then runs back out and around the yard to the reversing loop on the patio.

The plan allows main line operations from Cranis (inside the garage) through Cranis Junction to El Patio, with a branch line from the main line at Cranis Junction to South Eats. Modelers refer to this particular plan's schematic path as an *out-and-back* or *point-to-loop* with the junction allowing a choice of two points of origin for the trains (Cranis or South Eats).

ROBERT TREAT'S ROCK SHELF LINE

Robert Treat, like Herb Chaudiere, prefers his LGB equipment to look like part of a full-sized industrial railroad or branch line rather than a decorative part of the garden. Robert was lucky enough to have a 6- x 50-foot shelf sitting at the base of the cliff that rose from his back yard in Southern California. The

Garden Railway or Outdoor Railroading?

An outdoor railroad seeks to reproduce the appearance and/or operations of a real railroad. Scale foliage is sought; real railroad features (industries, towns, mountains, classification yards), reduced to scale models, help to determine track configurations. Equipment is chosen for fidelity to a real railroad or to a believable fiction, and usually is weathered for more realism.

Garden railways are decorative parts of a garden. Foliage need not be to scale; garden features (plantings, walks, benches, and fountains) provide the visible reasons for track configuration. Equipment is chosen for its aesthetic quality rather than prototype fidelity, and usually is clean and bright for visual appeal.

The difference is not which is more important, the back yard environment or the trains, but whether you want to base your layout on real railroad scenes or horticultural aesthetics.

shelf was about three feet above the back yard lawn and was an obvious place to build a model railroad. It was a train table complete with scenery just waiting for the trains.

But the train table was not made simply by dropping the track on the dirt shelf. The right of way for the track was marked out using both sectional track curves as templates for the roadbed location and a compass made of string and a stake to mark out some broader curves. For leveling to the proper grade, the roadbed was then either cut a bit deeper or the shallow areas were filled with pea-sized gravel to raise the track up from the shelf. He also added a few rocks and built as many bridges as the deeper dips in the shelf could justify (in places too deep for cuts and fills that "needed" crossing on a bridge.) The resulting layout is incredibly realistic, all the more because you can view it from track level without the need to lay your head on the ground.

Robert repainted the locomotives with Floquil model railroad paints and an artist's airbrush. The weathering is also Floquil paint, but with about nine parts thinner to one part paint, to create a thin wash. He also powdered some artist's pastel chalks and dusted it on the cars for a dirty effect (see Chapter 12). The locomotive (pictured in Color Plate 13) does NOT have smoke units in operation; he used cotton, dyed black and moved during the photographic exposure, to create fake smoke effects.

The scenes on Robert Treat's layout are very realistic, but they are attainable on just about any outdoor model railroad. You might not want to haul in an entire cliff's worth of dirt or rocks, and you might have to settle for track on the ground rather than on a shelf. But anyone can bring in piles of dirt, compact them with water and tamping, and create cuts similar to Robert's — which is what Norm Grant is doing in his relatively flat backyard. And the authentic looking equipment on Robert Treat's system can be duplicated more easily and cheaply than the terrain. The equipment and the track can be made to look more realistic with simple painting effects.

PETE THORP'S
LAGUNA & PIEDRAS GRANDE RAILWAY

In contrast to Robert Treat's railroad, Pete Thorp's, like those of Gary Nelson and David Charles, is a true garden railway. Pete planned the garden as an integral part of the railroad; the space had previously been filled with bare lawn. The layout occupies the areas just in front of a 72- x 35-foot long L of fence. The 35-foot portion is shown in Color Plate 16.

Pete used a 4 mil plastic sheet beneath the entire railroad area. That was covered with topsoil native to the central California area. The track was positioned, and the route marked with surveyor's stakes, placed about three feet apart. The stakes were then driven into the ground until the top of the stake was a little above where the bottom of the track would be. Pete could then use a level and an 8-foot board to adjust the heights of the tops of the stakes to provide a roadbed with a maximum grade of 1-1/2 percent.

The track was then laid on tamped-down topsoil and *ballast* with the chip-and-seal granite used for paving. The coarse texture of the chips was later softened with Gran-I-Grit, one of the brands of roughage sold by feed supply stores. The roughage washes away and must be replaced once a year for realism.

A believer in no-stall operation, Pete bridges every single track joint with a piece of flexible wire soldered to the rails on either side of the metal rail joiners. The rail joiners allow the rail to expand and contract slightly since, in time, they can wear or bend enough to leave a gap, or accumulate a layer of oxide that will not allow the electrical current to flow consistently. The jumper wires maintain electrical continuity long after the rail joiners are oxidized.

The track plan for the Laguna & Piedras Grande Railway includes a large oval around the entire 72- x 35-foot perimeter. A smaller oval, folded back over itself, lies inside one of the ends of the outer oval.

Two trains can operate independently on the two ovals. Pete uses a pair of Model Rectifier power packs with 501 throttles, one for each oval.

DAVID CHARLES' POOLSIDE LAYOUT

David Charles and his wife commissioned Norm Grant to create their LGB layout for them. He designed, engineered, and laid the track for them, and Mrs. Charles created the landscaping and designed the rock garden. When he began, an existing garden and shrubs already stood beside the edges of the pool deck in their back yard. The track runs along two sides of the back yard, skirting the pool deck and running along the fence. It forms a simple oval, bent so that one end extends out onto the pool deck near the patio, while the other end, by the fence, is hidden behind bushes near the pool heater and the dog house. There is a single passing siding at midpoint, to park a second train; there is room to expand with one or two more sidings.

The track work is all LGB with a few curves formed from flex track using the Larry Lindsay rail-bending tool to keep it from twisting. When rail is bent into a horizontal curve, because it has a thicker cross section at the bottom than at the top and is thinnest in the middle, it tends to twist like the rotation of a driveshaft. Pre-bending the rail with the rail-bending tool eliminates the need for rigid support that twisted rail must have. (The process is described in Chapter 3.)

The track is laid in scooped-out trenches about 6 inches wide and 2 inches deep with 4 mil sheet plastic placed in the bottom of the trench to stop weed growth. The trench is partially filled with the sand/clay mixture, which when hardened holds the track in place.

The high points of the Charles' layout are a pair of all wood bridges — a Howe truss bridge (Color Plate 18) and a curved trestle (Color Plate 19). Both the bridges were made to order by Kenosha Railway Supply from pine assembled with metal bolts, nuts, and threaded rods just as on the real bridges. Structures include a 907 Pola brand Silverton railroad station and a 923 Pola American prototype water tower. The locomotives and rolling stock are both American and European prototype models. The 2085D LGB *Mallet* 0-6-6-0 *articulated* locomotive, a Southern German Railway Company prototype, is particularly impressive rounding the broad curves through the garden scenery. (See Color Plate 20.) Mrs. Charles is cultivating a collection of miniature plants to complement the trains.

Chapter 3
Basic Track Assembly and Maintenance

LGB track is a large-scale version of the sectional track that has been used for decades on HO and N scale train sets. The LGB track, however, uses special plastic that will not be damaged by severe changes in weather or by sunlight. It is truly all-weather track, suitable for use indoors or outdoors in any season.

Expanding Track Plans

Any single route that a train can run without backing up can be expanded by inserting equal straight sections in the right places. To find the right places:

1. The inserted tracks must be exactly parallel to each other.

2. There must be a net total of 180 degress of curvature (six 1100s or 1500s, eight 1600s) between the two insertion points. (Count turns one way as positive, turns the other way as negative.) Actually 1 and 2 are equivalent requirements —either both are true or both are false. Checking both helps prevent error.

3. Trace the route from insertion point A to insertion point A1. All track that connects to your route between those two points must be able to move as a single unit with the route when it is moved to allow the insertions; that is, these connecting tracks must not join to part of the layout outside the route.

4. A common exception to step 3 occurs when the connecting track is a parallel siding that spans the route's insertion point. In this case, simply cut the connecting track, the siding, right beside the insertion point in the route, and make a third equal insertion there.

5. Once a first expansion has been made, other expansions may be added in the enlarged plan, following the same rules.

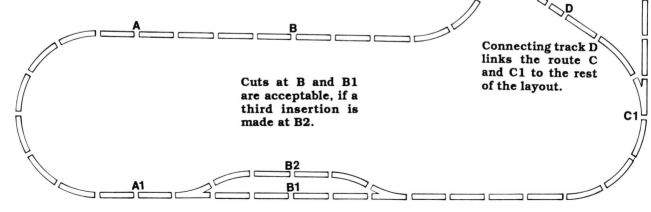

Insertions at C and C1 will work, but not at C and C2.

Connecting track D links the route C and C1 to the rest of the layout.

Cuts at B and B1 are acceptable, if a third insertion is made at B2.

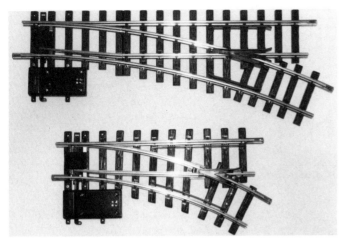

The LGB longer, more gradual 1615N turnout and the 1205N turnout.

The LGB 1226 electromechanical double-slip switcher (turnout).

TRACK ASSEMBLY

The track plans in this chapter will help to explain the geometry of the LGB track system. The various pieces are designed, like interchangeable pieces in a jigsaw puzzle, to fit tightly together. The geometry of the system allows you to add straight tracks in parallel pairs (on opposite sides of the circle) to expand a circle into an oval, and an oval into a square or a rectangle of any size.

The LGB turnouts and *crossings* are also designed to interchange with a standard piece of straight or curved track (depending on the particular turnout). This makes it possible to build a simple layout and to add turnouts later by pulling a single piece of track from the layout and replacing it with a turnout. Adding a *stub siding* to a circle, or a *passing siding* to a straight main line, is easy.

When curves are involved, tying the siding back into the main is more complicated, as is closing an irregular loop of track. A variety of special short *make-up tracks* sections can help.

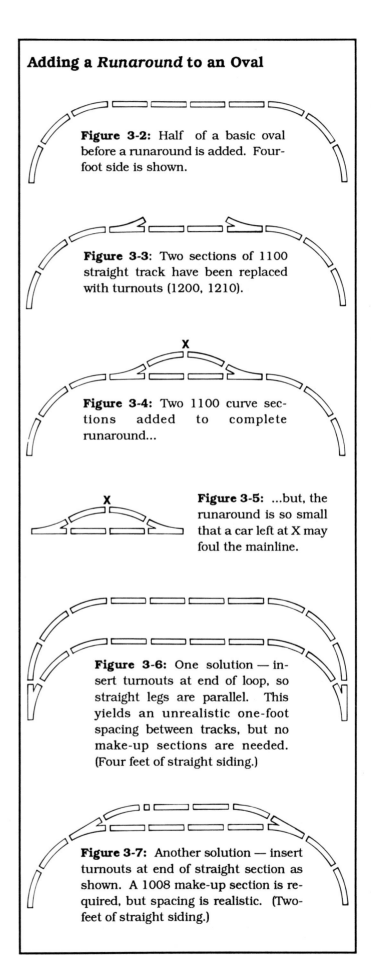

Adding a *Runaround* to an Oval

Figure 3-2: Half of a basic oval before a runaround is added. Four-foot side is shown.

Figure 3-3: Two sections of 1100 straight track have been replaced with turnouts (1200, 1210).

Figure 3-4: Two 1100 curve sections added to complete runaround...

Figure 3-5: ...but, the runaround is so small that a car left at X may foul the mainline.

Figure 3-6: One solution — insert turnouts at end of loop, so straight legs are parallel. This yields an unrealistic one-foot spacing between tracks, but no make-up sections are needed. (Four feet of straight siding.)

Figure 3-7: Another solution — insert turnouts at end of straight section as shown. A 1008 make-up section is required, but spacing is realistic. (Two-feet of straight siding.)

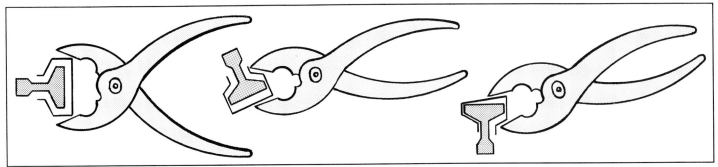

Figure 3-8: Use pliers to squeeze the rail joiners tight against the track.

Each LGB track section has a rail joiner on one end of each piece of rail; if you look out from the center toward one end of the section, the left-hand rail has the joiner. The rail joiners slide over the base *flanges* of the rail on the adjoining track section to lock that track into alignment in all directions. They also provide electrical continuity from one section to the next. Many modelers supplement this electrical connection with jumper wires (see Chapter 9), especially on large outdoor layouts.

Make-Up Tracks

1102:	15 degrees (one-half 1100)
1104:	7.5 degrees (one-quarter 1100)
1004:	41 mm
1005:	52 mm
1007:	75 mm
1008:	82 mm
1009:	88-120 mm

25 mm is approx. 1 inch
300 mm is approx. 1 foot

The rail joiners must be removed from the rail when installing a 5026 insulating joiner. Use a small screwdriver to pry between the vertical inside *web* and the inside edges of the rail joiner. Slide the rail joiner off, unhooking the vertical tab from the roadbed. To install a rail joiner, on a 1000/5 *flex-track* or a rail you have cut, use pliers to squeeze the base flanges, to pull the sides of the rail joiner together. Use the pliers, again, to squeeze the rail joiners tightly onto the top and bottom of each of the base flanges of the rail. (See Figure 3-8.)

TRACK ALIGNMENT

LGB offers an 1150 locking pin to lock the ties of one track section to the ties of another. This can help to keep the sections from working apart while in use. Remember, however, that the joints between sections are the weakest parts of the track. All considerations of realism aside, the track cannot, for example, be suspended across a chasm and supported by just the rail joiners — a bridge or board must support the track at the joint. (Real rail and ties, of course, cannot support themselves at any point.)

Vertical misalignment can often be a nagging and seemingly invisible cause of derailments. Check the **vertical alignment** by laying the side of your head on the floor or ground beside the track. Close one eye so the eye nearest the floor is open to sight down the SIDES of the rail to look for any sharp up or down angles at the rail joiners. If you find any, bend the track at the joint gently and add any supports that are needed to shim the track upward. Shim it up at the joint for a dip; shim it on either side of the joint — along the track toward the next joint — to correct a hump at the joint itself. You can use strips of cardboard for an indoor layout, and dirt or ballast for an outdoor layout, to shim the track up.

The 1150 track clips can be used to keep track joints from creeping apart.

For **horizontal alignment**, use the same method of laying your head down and sighting down the rails with the eye nearest the ground. This time, lay your head on the track and look down the TOPS of the rails. If there is any jog to the left or right at the joints, you may need to add or remove some sections of track to correct the alignment. First, however, be certain that every single track joint is tight so the ends of the rails butt snugly together. If there is still one area of misalignment, then you have somehow changed the geometry of the LGB system and the track arrangement must be altered slightly by inserting make-up tracks or by removing a section and cutting it to a shorter length.

Sometimes, simply adding one of the short curved track sections (1102 or 1104) or the very short straight track sections (1004, 1005, 1007, or 1008) will correct the problem. Try the short curve and the short straight sections on opposite sides of an oval or loop to determine their effect on the track alignment. Sometimes, the expandable section (1009) can be inserted and the length adjusted with its dial. Turning the dial telescopes the track, making it longer or shorter.

USING LGB FLEXIBLE TRACK

LGB offers 1.5 meter sections of 1000/5 brass rail with separate pieces of 1000/3 plastic ties. It takes two lengths of 1000/5 rail and five pieces of *tie-strip* (1000/3) to make 1.5 meters of track. Rail joiners (1000/1) are also available separately.

The 1009 expandable section can be telescoped from this 120 mm length down to as short as 88 mm (about 1-1/4 inches) by turning the knob.

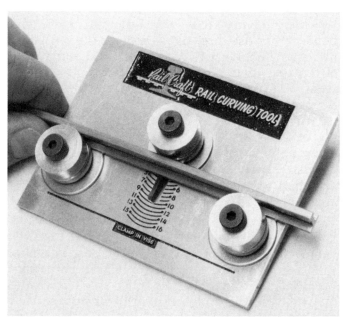

Pull the rail through the rail bender tool to produce a smooth, kink-free curve before installing the ties.

LGB calls the tie-strips "flexible" and they are; you can bend the lengths of ties right or left to any curve, from a 23-5/8 inch radius (to match the tightest — 1100 — curved track sections) on up, or just use them as-is for longer stretches of straight track. In fact, you can make curves tighter than standard, although you won't be able to run all equipment on a substandard curve. Short two-axle cars (i.e. 3012) and short two-axle engines (i.e. 2010D) can be operated on curves, without kinks, as tight as 16 inches in radius. A small engine by itself will run on even tighter curves.

The LGB rails, however, unlike the tie-strips, are certainly NOT flexible. If you want to use the "flexible" track on a curve, whatever the size, you MUST prebend the rails. If you don't, the rail will twist as you bend it, and may tear the tie-strip rail clamps. Twisted rail is a tracklayer's nightmare. And on tight curves, it will probably kink.

Using a Rail Bender

Start with the center roller moved just 1/16 inch in from no bend at all, and pull the rail through the rollers to get the first slight bend.

Move the roller another 1/16 inch inward and pull the rail through again.

Repeat the process, moving the center roller about 1/16 inch each time until you get the precise bend or curve in the rail you want.

Remember that the inside rail will always have a smaller radius than the outside rail.

Railcraft, Larry Lindsay, and other firms offer rail benders that use three rollers to force the rail gently into a broad curve with ALL of the bend in the sides of the rail, maintaining the vital horizontal alignment. The bender must be adjusted by trial and error, although there are usually some rough guidelines about what kind of radius you obtain by setting the center roller in the positions indicated. The screw adjustment of the middle roller on the more expensive Larry Lindsay rail bender is less likely to slip than a friction lock, and makes finer adjustments of radius easier to make and duplicate. After the rails are curved, the flexible tie-strips can be slipped onto the rail base.

The ends of the rails will have to be cut to join them to standard track sections (1000, 1100, 1205, etc.), because the process of bending the two rails into curves will leave the outer rail shorter than the inner rail. The inner rail needs to be cut to match the standard track. (Adding a short rail to the outer track, also possible, increases the number of rail joints and is more work.)

The 1000/5 rails slide easily into the 1000/3 tie-strips to make 1.5 meter long straight track sections.

If, however, you are using several sections of flexible track end to end, don't bother equalizing the rail lengths until you need to join them to a standard track section. The resulting offset of rail joints will produce slightly stronger track work because the weakest points of the rail, the joints, will be staggered. Just remember to put the flexible ties onto the rails before adding the rail joiners.

Fitting the joiners in the middle of a tie-strip may require a little plastic surgery with a sharp hobby knife.

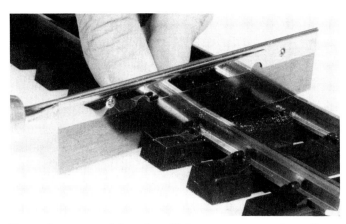

Use a Zona razor (shown) or X-Acto saw to cut the rails as indicated in the text.

To cut the metal rail, use a hacksaw or a modeler's razor saw like those sold by X-Acto and Zona. The finer teeth of the razor saw produce fewer metal burrs. The edges of the cut end of the rail must be filed smooth after using either saw. The base and web of the rail need to be free of burrs to allow the rail joiner to slide into place. The top or head of the rail must also be smooth so it does not interfere with the rolling of wheel flanges and tires. Roughness not severe enough to cause derailment can chip plastic wheels and wear them down rapidly.

Do not attempt to correct misalignments in the joints of flexible track by bending the track into a new position and holding it there with spikes or nails — it will eventually spring back out of alignment. Take the time to add or remove small sections of track, as described earlier, to get the horizontal alignment perfect; shim for vertical alignment. When adjusting flexible track, take at least one section apart and run BOTH rails through the rail bender once or twice until they assume the shape needed to produce perfect track alignment.

Some model railroad books suggest banking curves so the outside rail is about a scale 6 inches (a tad over 1/4 inch, in LGB's scale) higher than the inside rail. The real railroads do that, especially on main line trackage. It is difficult to maintain a smooth vertical transition from having both the right and left rails perfectly level from side to side, to raising just the outer rail through the curve. If you want to take the time to make a gentle vertical bend in that outer rail, you can achieve the banked curve, a process real railroads call "superelevation." Some operators feel a fast train looks better leaning inward as it speeds around a curve. But from an operating standpoint it is definitely NOT worth the trouble, especially since there's a good chance you'll bend some of the straight track into side-to-side horizontal misalignment.

TRACK MAINTENANCE

The LGB books suggest oiling the brass rails with either pure petroleum jelly (like Vaseline) or a mixture of kerosene (they call it by the British term, "paraffin") and oil. It has been the experience of some operators in this country that this does not work well on either indoor or outdoor layouts in America. The oily film attracts dust and dirt outdoors. Some American modelers use Wahl-brand hair clipper oil, a triply refined, very light oil sold at many shaver repair shops and barber shops. The oil does not increase electrical contact, but it does slow oxidation, the main rail contact problem, both by coating the surface and by reducing sparks that pit the railhead. (Rough surfaces oxidize faster.) But oiling rail is not common in any scale larger than O scale.

Some modelers have reported successful results, especially when doing maintenance after a long winter of no operations, using one of the various compounds sold by electronics hobby stores (like Radio Shack and Allied) as electrical contact cleaner. The fluid must be poured or sprayed onto a rag and wiped over the rails. First, however, the rails should be wiped clean with a heavy-duty cotton rag to remove any dust or dirt or debris.

Model railroad stores also sell a small abrasive rubber eraser, called a "Bright Boy," that can be rubbed along the tops of the rails to clean dirt, oil, and oxide. The inside top corner of the railhead is the point where the wheels make most electrical contact; be sure to polish there.

An excellent product for removing pine sap (or any tree sap) from the rail heads is the pretroleum-based lanolin hand cleaner that auto mechanics use. Put it on a cloth and rub lightly until the sap comes off. Wipe the residue off with a clean cloth or paper towels. Sap can also be removed by using a fine (200-400 grit) sandpaper, followed by a fine steel wool to polish the rail. Any loose particles of the steel wool that break off should be removed from the rails; however, there is no chance for the particles to be attracted by the magnets in the engine motors since the LGB motors, unlike other train models, are sealed off with a metal jacket. (If other engine brands are used, be sure to check that the motors are sealed before using steel wool.)

When exposed to the oxygen in the air, brass forms a cupric oxide that is an effective electrical insulator. The trick to cleaning rails is to remove that oxide without creating minute scratches that seem to encourage the formation of even more cupric oxide. Do NOT, then, try to clean the rails by scraping them with a knife, a file, or emery paper, because scratches will be left in the tops of the rails.

LGB offers a couple of track cleaning devices; the number 5005 device places a pair of abrasive blocks over each rail. Mounted beneath one of the cars and pushed around the layout, it can rub the track clean. As a substitute for the abrasive blocks on track cleaners like this, modelers have used hardboard, such as Masonite, with the rough side down. LGB also offers a hand-held 5004 track cleaning device that works like the "Bright Boy" eraser to rub the tops of the rails clean. An American firm, Two Point Five Models, makes a clever track cleaning device that mounts a pair of rotating abrasive disks, designed not to damage the rails, beneath a tender or freight car. The motion of the car down the track spins the abrasive wheel to scrub the track clean (see photo on page 82).

Chapter 4
Basic Track Plans for LGB

One of the many joys of LGB trains is a track system that actually functions: the track sections are strong, fit tightly together, and align properly. The track, like the trains, is substantial. LGB advertising in the 1970s even included a photo of an elephant with its foot on the track.

The track plans in this chapter use *sectional track*, a good choice when designing a small layout. In addition to the sectional track, LGB offers 1.5 meter (5 foot) lengths of flexible track that are helpful when building large outdoor or indoor layouts.

Track plans fall into types, classified by the pattern of *main line* routing. Assuming you don't try to squeeze track into spaces too small for it, and that you leave enough room for the cars and engines to get by furniture, trees, and each other, your only track designing problem will be getting a track to connect back onto itself. If your plan is *point-to-point*, your only fitting challenges will be getting runaround tracks (passing sidings) to match up when they return to the main line. (See Chapter 3.) If your route is continuous, or you have a reversing loop as in an out-and-back plan, then you have to watch the total degrees of curvature, so the tracks you want to join don't end up skewed with lateral displacement. Fortunately, when getting started you don't have to master geometrical theory. You can design your own track plans for LGB track and be certain of perfect alignment of the sections, especially when working with the smaller curves, if you understand the basic geometry of the system and know which parts are interchangeable. Once you know that the curved leg of a turnout* can replace a curved section of track, or that adding a 1015 to the 1015T you used for electrical reasons makes the two the equivalent of a 1000 straight, you're on your way. (See Chapter 9

---

*In referring to track, "switch" and "turnout" can be used interchangeably, although "turnout" is preferred.

for uses of the insulating tracks 1015U and 1015T; they are shown where needed in the plans in this chapter.)

For curves and turnouts, LGB offers two sets of sections, with somewhat different geometry: the small curves and turnouts (1100, 1500, 1200 series) and the large (1600 series). Their geometries are not quite the same. (For an example of a plan using the large turnouts, see Figure 5-4 on page 40.)

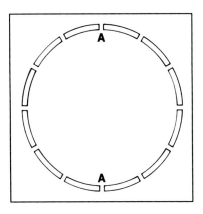

Figure 4-1: Single track loop or circle, 4'6" x 4'6". Track needed: twelve 1100s. Circle radius, center-to-center: 60 cm (approx. 24 inches). 1100 section: 30 degrees. When calculating grades, treat the 12-1/3 inch 1100 sections as though 1-foot long; the small margin will help compensate for the increased drag of the curve.

EXPANDING THE BASIC LAYOUT

The circle of track shown in Figure 4-1 is included in LGB starter sets. That circle can be expanded into an oval (as in 4-17) by inserting matching-length pairs of straight track sections at any opposite points, such as A and A. (See Chapter 3.) The length of those matching pairs of straights can be anything from 41 mm (1004) on up to combinations of the long 1.5-meter straight sections you can make with the flexible track (1000/5 rail, 1005/3 ties, 1005/1 joiners).

Main Line Routing Types

Plans are classified according to the way the main line runs.

POINT-TO-POINT: These plans are point-to-point because the train must stop in order to return to its starting point. (Figures 4-2, 4-3, and 4-4)

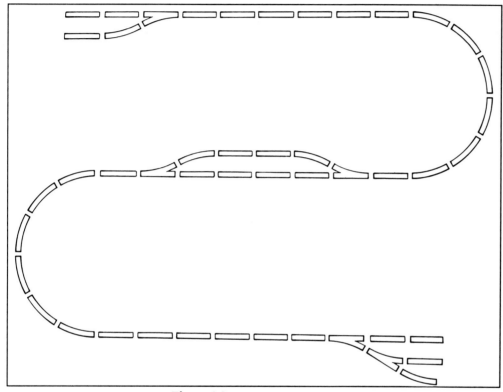

Figure 4-2

Figure 4-4

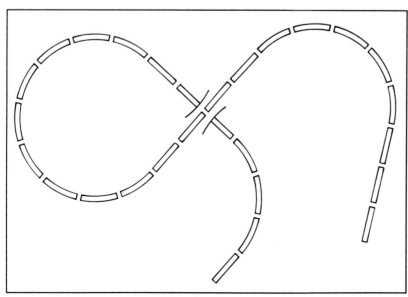

Figure 4-3

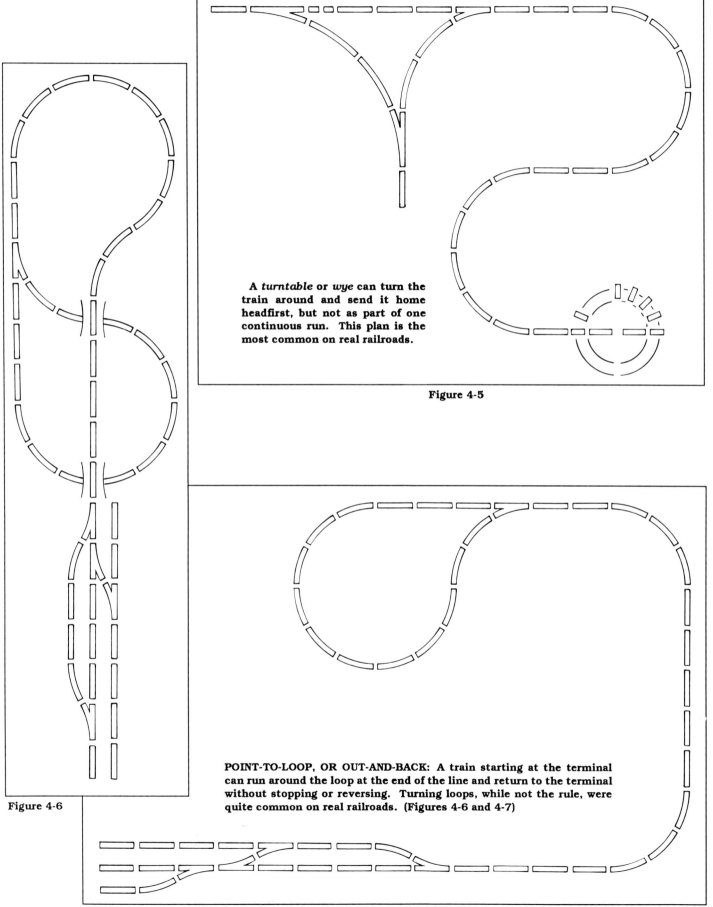

A *turntable* or *wye* can turn the train around and send it home headfirst, but not as part of one continuous run. This plan is the most common on real railroads.

Figure 4-5

Figure 4-6

POINT-TO-LOOP, OR OUT-AND-BACK: A train starting at the terminal can run around the loop at the end of the line and return to the terminal without stopping or reversing. Turning loops, while not the rule, were quite common on real railroads. (Figures 4-6 and 4-7)

Figure 4-7

LOOP-TO-LOOP: **The loops in this and the preceding type require special electrical treatment (see Chapter 9). The pattern works best if the run from loop to loop is long. The loops themselves may be side by side. (Figure 4-8)**

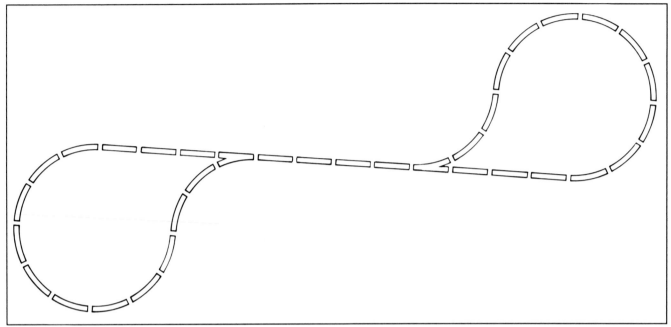

Figure 4-8

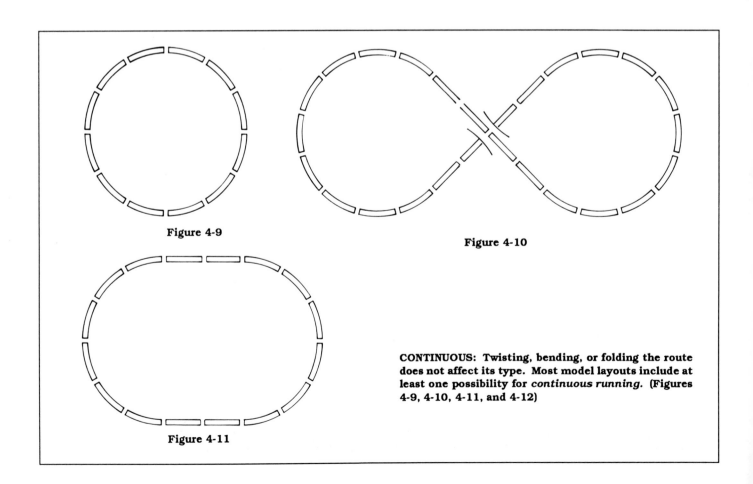

Figure 4-9

Figure 4-10

Figure 4-11

CONTINUOUS: Twisting, bending, or folding the route does not affect its type. Most model layouts include at least one possibility for *continuous running*. (Figures 4-9, 4-10, 4-11, and 4-12)

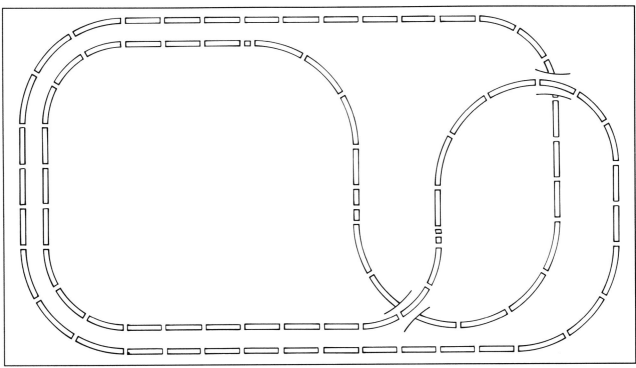

Figure 4-12

THE GEOMETRY OF BASIC LGB TRACK

STRAIGHT TRACK SECTIONS:	SMALL RADIUS SECTIONS:	LARGE RADIUS SECTIONS:
1000: 300 mm length	1100: 30 degrees, 60 cm radius	1600: 22.5 degrees,117.5 cm radius
1060: 600 mm length	1500: 30 degrees, 77.5 cm radius	1605, 1615: turnouts
1015: 150 mm length	1200, 1205, 1210, 1215 turnouts:	440 mm straight leg
	300 mm straight leg	22.5 degree, 117.5 cm radius curved leg
	30 degree, 60 cm radius curved leg	

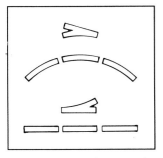

Figures 4-13 and 4-14: The small 1200 series turnouts have a curved section which can replace an 1100 curved track and a straight section which can replace a 1000 straight track.

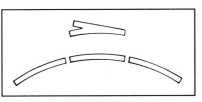

Figure 4-15: The curved section of a large 1605/1615 turnout can replace a 1600 curved section.

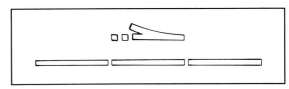

Figure 4-16: To replace a 1060 straight section with 1605/1615 you need to add make-up sections (1009, plus either 1004 or 1003 for an exact fit; two 1008s are close enough).

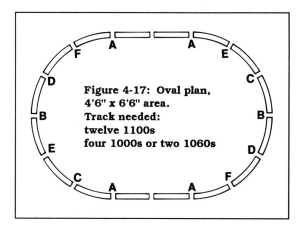

Figure 4-17: Oval plan, 4'6" x 6'6" area. Track needed: twelve 1100s four 1000s or two 1060s

The basic oval (Figure 4-17) can be expanded to a rectangle or square by inserting track at the points marked B-B and into a diamond or lozenge by inserting equal straights at C-C, D-D, E-E, or F-F; an octagonal-shaped plan could be made out of a circle of large radius sections (sixteen 1600s) by inserting matching-length pairs of straight track sections between each 1600 curve. Just follow the rules given in Chapter 3 (page 21).

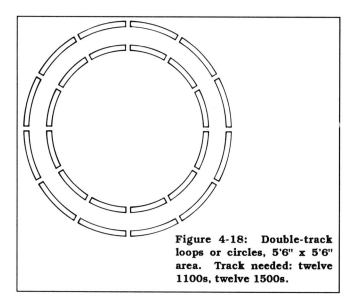

Figure 4-18: Double-track loops or circles, 5'6" x 5'6" area. Track needed: twelve 1100s, twelve 1500s.

Remember, it is essential that both rails of any two joined track sections butt firmly together without any sudden angles. Misalignment at these track section joints can result in derailments and generally poor operation. Use the make-up sections listed in Chapter 3 (p. 23) for adjustments.

TWO-TRAIN OPERATIONS

The simplest way to operate two trains is to build two separate layouts, one inside the other as shown in Figure 4-18. If you want the two trains to be

Problems in Layout Design

When planning layouts, remember:

1. Cars overhang the track: the track is only 3-1/2 inches wide, but the cars are wider. And not all cars are equal width. On straight tracks, allow 2-1/2 inches each side of track center.

2. Cars overhang farther on curves: a 48-inch diameter circle needs 3-1/2 inches more on each side for the cars to clear obstacles such as another train on a parallel track or a tunnel gate.

3. The 48-inch diameter circle will not fit into a 48-inch wide space: the diameter is track center to track center, not outer edge to outer edge.

4. 330 degrees do not make a complete circle. Count your curves.

Parking Locomotives

If two locomotives are on the same circuit, being run by the same power pack, an effect of separate control is obtained by parking one while the other runs. There are three ways to park a locomotive, all of which cut off its electricity or reduce the power below starting point:

1. Some LGB locomotives (mostly ones of European prototype) won't begin to roll until nine volts is applied to the track. In the meantime, more normal locomotives can be operated. With "*EAV*," Lehmann's former label for locomotives that take more current to start than others, they will sit at a station while the other locomotive does switching moves. When the power is turned up so that both are moving, they must both go in the same direction; usually, you would park the switcher after it does its work before starting the EAV locomotive on its way down the main. Lehmann no longer stresses this feature, since others are more satisfactory.

2. Most Lehmann locomotives now come with switches in the cab that allow the locomotive to be turned fully off, or partially off with lights and smoke working but the wheels not rolling.

3. Insulation in the track rails (1015T, 1015U, 5026) can be used to remove power from selected track areas. With switches operated either by manual control (e.g., 5080), or by track contact (1700, 1701), or by the motion of the train through the turnout (with 1203 attached), such insulated sections offer a wide range of possibilities. You can make your own on-off controls with toggle switches sold by firms like Radio Shack and Allied. Whenever two trains are moving, they will go in the same direction.

controlled separately, you need two power packs or transformers, each connected to one circle of track.

It is possible to operate two locomotives from a single power pack but both must start and stop at the same time, which is not very exciting for the operator. Alternative possibilities for operating two trains from one power pack include different ways of parking one while the other runs.

Another possibility for two-train control is LGB's system of working overhead or *catenary* wires for *trolley* or *interurban* trains. It allows them to be operated on a separate circuit via the overhead wires. Running one locomotive from the overhead wire (plus one rail of the track) and another from the two track rails gives genuinely independent control when two power packs are used. A limitation with the two packs is that engines getting their power from overhead wire cannot be turned and run in the opposite direction on the same track (unless a block control system is used). So far, trolley and electric locomotives of European prototypes only are being made by LGB.

The method most common in smaller scales is block control, in which the layout is divided into electrically isolated units; electrical switches for each track block determine which power pack is feeding current to it, so that operator A can run a train in blocks 8 and 9 while operator B is running a train in blocks 4 and 5. The wiring is fairly complicated. (See Chapter 9, Figure 9-12.)

Installing Battery Power

Rechargeable nicad batteries can be assembled in 12 to 18 volt packs, loaded into a high-sided 4021 gondola, and pulled by the engine they power. The engine must be rewired so only battery power, not track power, goes to the motor. Lehmann locomotives contain brass strips for electrical interconnection that make intercepting the current at the wheels tricky; the best place to cut the circuit is at the motor itself. To do this, disassemble the drive chassis to get at the motor. Attach wire leads from the battery system to the motor contacts, and wrap them in electrical tape or some other insulator. Routing the wires is up to you, and will require a notch here, a hole there.

Yet another method of independent two-train operation is to power one train by a battery in the train. If you want the locomotive to do anything besides run in one direction at full speed, you will want a radio-controlled speed controller of the sort sold for use in model boats or model cars. The on-board unit should fit easily with the battery into

Crossings

The 30-degree crossing (1300) is equivalent to, or more than, a 1000 straight, depending on which leg is traversed; it is not symmetrical. However, it can join two 1100 circles in a figure eight.

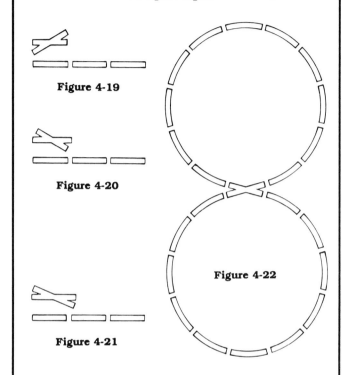

Figure 4-19

Figure 4-20

Figure 4-21

Figure 4-22

The 22-1/2 degree double slip switch (a switchable crossing; 1226) is more than a 1000 when going straight across. It can join two 1600 circles in a figure eight that allows staying at one end or weaving back and forth.

an LGB car. Follow the directions that come with the radio and speed-control.

The most enjoyable method of operating several trains is a carrier/command-control system such as those sold by Keller as the Onboard system and by PSI as the Dynatrol system. These systems use walk-around throttles on wire tethers connecting them to special power packs. Each locomotive is fitted (usually by the operator) with an electronic receiver. A steady current is fed to the rails and electronic signals change the current from slow to fast or from forward to reverse inside the locomotive itself. The beauty of these systems is that you can control trains on the same track independently. With sidings for the second class train to duck into as the first class train roars by on the main, two trains can run in opposite directions on the same loop of track. (For more detailed information, see Chapter 9.)

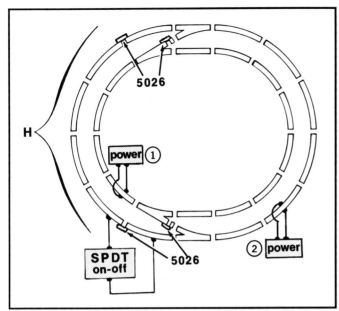

Figure 4-23: Double-track loops or circles with two cross-overs, 5'6" x 6'6" area. Track needed for inner loop: ten 1100s, two 1000s, one 1200 or 1205, one 1210 or 1215. Outer loop: twelve 1500s, one 1200 or 1205, one 1210 or 1215. Plus: two 1005s, four 5026s (less than one package) Note: you must use 5026 joiners in at least the outer rail of both 1005s for control of two-train operation.

THE BASIC TWO-TRAIN OVAL

The easiest to install and least expensive method of operating two trains at once is to give them two separate track systems so each can follow its own path without ever running into the other. A simple pair of track circles as shown in Figure 4-18 accomplishes this. It is easy to operate, but the results are a bit boring. If the plan is expanded with two pairs of turnouts as shown in Figure 4-23, then each of the two trains has an alternate route of either the inner or the outer oval. (However, this is not the easiest method of operating two trains.) One pair of turnouts would be enough to get the trains from one oval to the other, but they would have to back up to reverse the maneuver. Two pairs allow access to either oval from either direction; however, the two trains must be traveling in the same clockwise or counterclockwise direction.

BLOCK OR SECTION CONTROL

One power pack feeds current to the outer loop; a second feeds power to the inner loop. A 5026 plastic joiner insulates the outer rail of the 1005 short section in each *crossover*, keeping the two circuits separated. For the trains to swap ovals, at least one of the trains must be stopped. On this plan, a "holding" section has been included as the left-hand

half circle of the outer loop (H): plastic joiners in the outer rail at left electrically isolate that half circle. A wire across the *gap*, through an on-off switch (*SPDT*, for single pole, double throw, such as one of the switches in 5080), allows the current to be turned on or off. Turned on, it sends H the same current as the rest of the outer oval; turned off, H gets no current.

BASIC TWO-TRAIN INTERCHANGE WITH SECTION CONTROL

For both trains to be moving clockwise, the procedure for *interchanging* Train 1 from the outer oval with Train 2 on the inner oval proceeds as follows:

1. Stop Train 1 at H, and turn its on-off switch off.

2. Set one pair of turnouts for the crossover route.

3. Run Train 2 onto the outer oval with the inner power pack. When it stops halfway through the crossover, turn on the outer power pack, and run Train 2 all the way through the crossover onto the outer loop.

4. Turn on H's on-off switch, and with the outer pack, start both trains slowly clockwise around the outer oval.

5. When Train 2 enters H, after it has cleared the turnout behind it, turn H off.

6. As Train 1 approaches the turnout, set the turnouts for the crossover route, and run Train 1 into the oval.

7. When the train stops, turn on the inner pack, and run Train 1 the rest of the way into the inner oval.

8. Reset the crossovers for straight routing.

9. Turn H on; operate Train 1 on the inner oval with the inner power pack, and Train 2 on the outer oval with the outer power pack.

CREATING YOUR OWN TRACK PLANS

A good way to create a simple track plan is to use the actual sections of track. With this method you can be certain that each and every track section fits snugly with the next for perfect alignment.

An alternative method, especially for more complicated layouts, is to draw the track plan, to scale, on paper just as we have done in this chapter. Over a large area small bits of play may produce a noticeable net error in the layout. It is much easier to discover you don't have room for extra track before you buy it. You can also expand your basic layout to fit your dream plan when you have the time — or the money.

LGB offers a track planning *template* (1001) that includes all their track sections to a practical scale, for small layouts, of 1:10. Note that if your area is larger than seven feet by nine feet, you will need a piece of paper bigger than the standard 8-1/2 x 11".

Simply trace the outline of the track sections as described in the template's instructions. You must first draw a 1:10 scale plan of the space you have available, but there is a 1:10 scale along one side of the template, in meters, that will help. If you don't want to determine the size of your space in meters, do it in inches, using an inch ruler to lay it out on paper: a 12-1/2 foot room will be 150 inches, and will need a piece of paper on which you can mark off a 15-inch width for your 1:10 template track markings. (If the room were 152 inches, you would have to estimate two tenths of an inch.) Whether you measure your 1:10 plan in inches, meters, or cubits, once you have a one-tenth-size room plan, you can use the metric 10:1 template.

Most of the common LGB track sections and turnouts are used with the exception of the double slip switch (turnout 1226) and three-way turnout (shown in Chapter 3). These turnouts require special length sections to fit them into most plans. If you want to use them, you should also purchase the LGB-Information book (0026 or the newer 0028) to see the variety of track patterns and spacings that can be produced with these two turnouts. LGB catalogues also describe some of the track geometry.

SWITCHING LAYOUTS

A small point-to-point layout may either be a back and forth display, such as George Nachwalter's streetcar shuttling back and forth in front of *building flats* on an eight-inch shelf, or it will inevitably be a

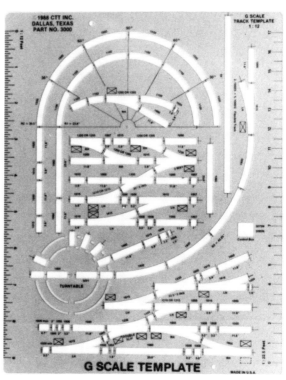

Track planning is made easier with a template. Pictured here is the G Scale Template made by CTT, Inc. LGB makes one also.

switching layout. If it is small, there will simply be no room for main line running.

Select your coupler type and brand. (See Chapter 10. If you use LGB hook-and-loop, you can uncouple manually with a narrow spatula by pushing down between the loop and the other car so it depresses the hook while you slowly move the engine away.) Then decide what length of car and engine you will typically run. The critical areas on a switching layout must be at least as long as one car plus the engine.

Nachwalter wall layout.   The scratch-built building flats are based on photographs of New Orleans prototypes.

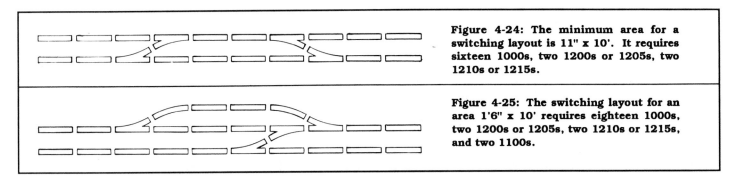

Figure 4-24: The minimum area for a switching layout is 11" x 10'. It requires sixteen 1000s, two 1200s or 1205s, two 1210s or 1215s.

Figure 4-25: The switching layout for an area 1'6" x 10' requires eighteen 1000s, two 1200s or 1205s, two 1210s or 1215s, and two 1100s.

Figure 4-24 is a minimum space switching layout that can provide a lot of operation on a shelf ten feet long and eleven inches wide. To maximize operational interest, some compromises have to be made. For example, rolling stock will overhang the shelf edge when operating on the trackage near the front. Also, many of the clearances are necessarily tight and require using smaller rolling stock, such as the 2010D and short cars like the 4030. Keep in mind that trains operating at the back of the layout must stay clear of the wall or back drop. Place the center of the rear track at least 3-1/2 inches from the wall for clearance. Also remember that the clearance between a siding and the main line diminishes at a turnout. Cars parked on a siding must be far enough away from the turnout to allow clearance for passing trains. Otherwise, they are said to "foul" the main line.

If you would rather use longer equipment, you can expand the plan by extending it 4-1/2 feet (adding length equally at the center and each end). This will allow the use of the 2028D Mogul and cars such as the 4068 D & R G W stock car. Your shortest train will be 3-1/2 foot long, so clearances should be maintained accordingly.

Operation consists of taking cars from a designated arrival site (where you place them by hand to start the session) and switching them into predetermined destinations. Imagine the back track to be the main line, and place arriving cars and the switcher there. If you wish, you can imagine the whole to be a tiny *branch* line terminal, and treat one end of the back track as a siding, which gives you three tracks on which to *spot* cars. (Spotting is placing a car at a specific location.) Since two turnouts will be *facing point* (that is, branching off in the same direction in which the train is headed), you will need to run around the cars one at a time to push them into those destinations.

Note that you can have two destinations per siding, one right at the switch, one at the stub end. Two industries per siding is common prototype practice. To keep them straight, you can put a colored or numbered *tab* on the track itself. If your shelf is twelve inches instead of eleven, put some building flats along the wall for the two sidings there. (Keep the track toward the front, so the cars overhang the shelf.) Until you have time to make better flats, "buildings" could just be pictures cut from a magazine.

Once you get the hang of spotting a couple of arrivals, add a car already sitting at a siding, pick it up (couple the engine to it), and return it to the original location. If your space is wider than a 12-inch shelf, you have some choices:

1. Replace tabs and flats with three-dimensional structures. Try scratch-building a small cattle pen (basically a fence with a ramp) which is easy to make.

2. Angle the sidings coming straight out of the turnouts, instead of having them parallel. They clear the main faster, giving you a little more free siding, and they look less like part of the main line.

3. Add additional sidings, coming off the runaround track.

4. For even more switching variety, see Figure 4-25. Its two sidings are a *switchback*. Plan to have spotting locations at both ends of the switchback, so that to get a car into the hole, you have to plan on clearing anything parked at the front end. You have room in 4-25 to expand, adding the sidings of 4-24 by replacing the two curved tracks in 4-25 with turnouts.

If your space is longer than ten feet, use the first three feet of the extra length, divided equally, to lengthen the three critical areas: the two stubs at the ends and the runaround in the middle.

Chapter 5
Advanced Track Plans

Eventually, most of us tire of seeing the train run around and around a simple circle or oval of track. Two trains, on two ovals, make operations much more interesting, but the joy of the hobby can be even greater thanks to a wide variety of potential track layouts that are easy to assemble, modify, enlarge, or completely rebuild with LGB sectional track. All you need is a smooth and level roadbed for the track. Many modelers who build outdoor layouts do not spike or nail the track in place even in the severe environment of the outside world.

EXPANDING COMPLEX TRACK PLANS

Earlier, in Chapter 4, you have seen that the basic circle of track can be greatly expanded by adding pairs of equal-length straight track sections at points where the track joints are parallel. With a complex plan, more than two tracks may have to be extended.

Consider Figure 5-1. Straights may be inserted, in matching pairs at the following places. A simple double insertion may be made at:

AA in the left loop;

AA in the right loop;

GG in the left loop;

D in the left loop, with either D1 or D2.

More complex triple insertions are possible at FFF, cutting through the cutoff track;

C in the left loop, C in the right loop, with C1 or C2 in the cutoff track.

Cutting through the cutoff track to expand is possible because the route from C on the left to C1 or C2 satisfies requirements 1 and 2 (described in Chapter 3: parallel cuts, separated by a net 180 degrees of curvature), and so does the route from C on the left to C on the right.

ENGINEER, DISPATCHER, OR SPECTATOR?

Model railroaders tend to have certain roles they like to play. These roles tend to influence layout design schemes. John Armstrong, the nationally known layout expert, classified the three basic types as engineer, dispatcher, and spectator.

The **engineer** imagines himself in the cab of his locomotive. He stays with the train as it travels. One of his primary interests is switching cars in and out of sidings, constantly changing the make-up of his train as he delivers and picks up imagined loads. A good layout for an engineer will have many destinations — and multiple sidings. One-train operation

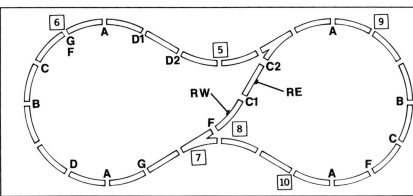

Figure 5-1: Small oval plan with reversing loop cutoff, 4'6" x 10'. Special wiring is required at RE and RW to control current direction in the cutoff track independently of current direction in the oval. There is no gain in using the reversing-track unit 1015K in the loop, since that would restrict travel at one end to one direction, making the reversing cutoff pointless. Track needed: twenty 1100s, one 1200 or 1205, one 1210 or 1215, four 1000s, and four 5026s (less than one pkg.)

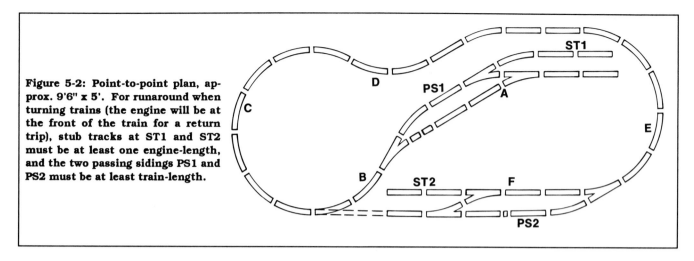

Figure 5-2: Point-to-point plan, approx. 9'6" x 5'. For runaround when turning trains (the engine will be at the front of the train for a return trip), stub tracks at ST1 and ST2 must be at least one engine-length, and the two passing sidings PS1 and PS2 must be at least train-length.

may be enough. As an engineer, he doesn't mind disconnecting his locomotive and running it around the train to work its way back up the track. A meandering point-to-point layout suits him fine.

The **dispatcher** imagines himself in a tower operating switches and signals, or in a more modern context, at a Centralized Traffic Control board doing the same thing electronically. He likes two things: multiple routings and complex junctions, both with lots of trains meeting and passing each other as he controls their destinies. The only sidings he cares about are passing sidings on the main line. A good layout for a dispatcher has the junctions and alternate routes he loves, and most important, the potential to run a number of trains at once; remote-control switches, command control, and tight timetables are his joy. His favorite layout is shaped like a mound of spaghetti.

The **spectator** likes to sit back and gaze at a beautiful scene through which trains roll untended by him. A good layout for a spectator includes continuous running routes he need not attend to; the routes may even be automated. Curves will be broad and sweeping. The track plan will be designed to afford him the best view from his accustomed chair. His layout is like a framed picture, and as such it may have an unattractive backside that no one ever sees.

POINT-TO-POINT OPERATIONS

Real railroads do not run around in circles. They haul commodities or passengers from one point to another; hence they are called "point-to-point." It is possible to modify an oval of LGB track to a plan similar to the point-to-point diagram in Figure 5-2. You then only need to imagine that points A and F are miles apart rather than just being on opposite sides of the table, or room, or backyard. If you build

this layout on a table, a backdrop at least head-high can be installed to run from midway between B and F to E, to prevent anyone from viewing the tracks and trains at A and at F at the same time — you would only be able to see A while standing beside that edge of the table. If the layout table is at chest height, a high mountain ridge or even a thick forest would adequately block a view of A from F.

You can also consider Figure 5-1 to be simply a schematic for a railroad that might meander all over your backyard. In a backyard layout, the trains might actually be going someplace — from, say, the patio door, around the periphery of the yard, to the back of the garage, to the opposite side of the swimming pool. With a route like that, you might even use the train to haul commodities like drinks and sandwiches from patio to pool.

One of the disadvantages of the point-to-point layout, to some model railroaders, is the need to rearrange the train completely every time it travels over the railroad, in order to get the engine at the front and any caboose at the rear. But for the would-be engineer, that is part of the joy. Although you can run the train forward from A to F (in Figure 5-2) and simply back it up to return from F to A, it is more interesting to put the locomotive at the front of the train for both trips. If you like to perform switching maneuvers, then this could be the most interesting aspect of the entire hobby. If you just want to see trains run, try another type of track plan that allows continuous running.

There is a passing siding at both A and at F on the point-to-point track diagram in Figure 5-2. When the train enters the trackage at F, locomotive first, the locomotive will uncouple and leave the train on the siding while it runs around on the track beside the train to couple onto what was the rear of the train. Every other trip the locomotive will operate with the tender, not the smokestack, at the front of the train. If you object to that, install turntables or wyes at both

A and F; or better, install a wye at one and a turntable at the other. Or find the space for a loop-to-loop layout.

CHAMELEON OPERATION

If you already have a loop layout, you do not have to tear it up for point-to-point operation. You can lap the miles in the morning and switch sidings in the afternoon. Simply imagine that the layout is point-to-point.

It doesn't matter whether the oval is simple or convoluted. A possible train routing in Figure 5-5 (see page 41) follows the sequence from 1 through 7,10, and 9, to 8, and repeats counterclockwise; 1 and 8 are imagined to be end-of-line terminals. On a simple oval, you could install a passing siding, which is a track that parallels the main line with a switch at both ends for entry or exit of trains from the main. Then designate one track of the siding as Town One (T1) and the other track of the siding as Town Two (T2). Operate trains from T1 to T2, stop, and rearrange the train so the locomotive is in front for the return trip, in the opposite direction.

LOOP-TO-LOOP OPERATIONS

If you might object to the need to rearrange the train at both ends of a point-to-point layout, consider the loop-to-loop design in Figure 5-3 as an alternative plan. With this plan the trains travel in the direction indicated by the arrows, beginning their journey at A and ending at F. This time, though, when the train from A reaches F it will already be headed, locomotive-first, for its return trip to A. Additional stub-ended or passing sidings can be added at A, F, or even between C and D for switching maneuvers to rearrange the train's cars.

The loop-to-loop plan has some shortcomings, especially for small layouts. It requires a lot of space, at least the equivalent of three circles side by side, and most of the trackage is only traveled once each trip between A and F and back again to A. The trackage between C and D is used only by trains traveling in both directions. This may not be a problem if the layout has a run from C to D of 100 feet or more. Basically, it is the type of plan that can be enlarged by inserting any length or shape of track between C and D to fit a large backyard outdoor layout. Note that the reversing loops at each end require special electrical handling (1015T, 1015K, or isolated reversing track or section; see Chapter 9); the current for every trip has to be reversed either by you, the operator, or by an automatic device.

OUT-AND-BACK OPERATION

It is also possible to combine the design aspects of the point-to-point layout with the loop-to-loop layout. You might, for example, decide that you would enjoy one terminal where the locomotive needs to run around the train on every trip. You might, then, decide to replace the loop from E to F in Figure 5-3 with a simple runaround or passing siding like the one at F in Figure 5-2. The layout would only consist of the trackage E D C and the reverse loop A B. Modelers call this point-to-loop design an out-and-back layout.

Trains start their journey at E on this shortened layout, travel around the reverse loop from A to B, pause for loading, unloading, or switching moves, and then return to E. The train is then rearranged, at E, to return to A, locomotive first. If you think about it, you will realize that the locomotive will operate tender first on every other round trip from E to A and back to E, unless a turntable or wye is used at E to turn the engine around.

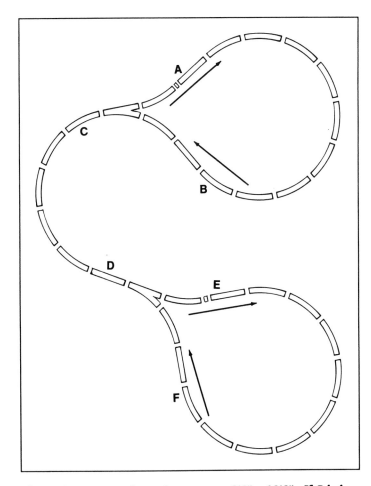

Figure 5-3: Loop-to-loop plan, approx. 8'6" x 10'3". If C is in a corner of a room, an access aisle should be left open between B and E toward C.

Herb Chaudiere's Cranis Garden Railway (see Figures 2-2 and 2-3 on pages 17-18) is an out-and-back with a second stub-ended terminal, giving trains exiting the loop a choice of two destination points: South Eats or Cranis. Since turntables at both Cranis and South Eats can turn the locomotives to head in the proper direction when the train is ready to leave town, there is no need for tender-first operations.

LAYOUTS PLANNED FOR OPERATION

The basic track plan in Figures 5-1, 5-4, and 5-5 includes a reversing loop cutoff track across the center of a bent oval. The plans allow out-and-back operation beginning, in Figure 5-1, with a train heading in a counterclockwise direction at 5. The train then proceeds around the oval through 6 and 7. You can then decide if the train should make a few more laps of the oval, traveling on from 7 through 10, 9, 5, 6, and 7, to add some distance to its run. When it does take the straight route through the turnout at 7, it will travel through 8, 9, and 10 to return to 7 heading in the opposite direction for its trip back to 5.

The train is now running clockwise. With this layout you have two choices for returning the train, now traveling clockwise around the oval, back to counterclockwise travel: you can add a pair of turn-outs to the tracks between 5 and 6 to make a passing siding like those at A and F in Figure 5-2, run the locomotive around the siding to the other end of the train, and begin the counterclockwise run of the preceding paragraph, but with the tender first. Or you can opt to make the train back up so it is now traveling counterclockwise, caboose first through the straight route of the turnout at 7, past 8, 9, and 10. The train can then be reversed into forward operation, and travel around the outer oval in its original counterclockwise direction, locomotive first. No additional turnouts are needed with this choice, unless you wanted them to hold a second train or to serve as industrial sidings.

The track plan in Figure 5-4 is nearly identical to the plan in Figure 5-1 except that this plan uses only the largest radius LGB curved track and turnouts. The trains look far more realistic on the larger curves. Note, however, that the space required is four times the area of the plan in Figure 5-1. The plan in Figure 5-1 could be placed on a table with either B end against the wall and access aisles along the remaining three sides: a peninsula design. The layout in Figure 5-4, however, is really too large for a single table. It would be better to build that layout on shelves around the walls of a room that is 10 feet 6 inches wide and at least 18 feet long. Many single-car garages are this size; so, of course, is half of a two-car garage. As always, the length can be extended with additional pairs of straight tracks, in-

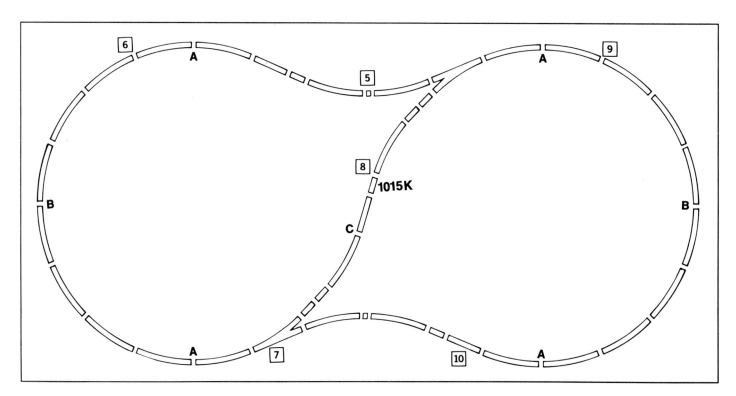

Figure 5-4: **Large oval plan with reversing loop cutoff, 10'3" x 18'. Unlike Figure 5-1, this plan has room for a 1015K in the reversing loop cutoff rather than the loop itself. The cutoff must always be traversed from left to right.**

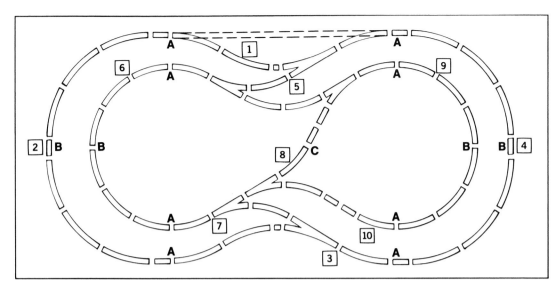

Figure 5-5: The "ultimate" small LGB layout, 6'4" x 11'8". All curves in the outer loop are 1500; the rest are all 1100. Note that because of the 1015K, the inner oval can only be traversed in a clockwise direction. The 1200 turnout leading to 8 should be left set to the straight leg into the cutoff. It is spring-loaded, so it will allow trains to exit from 10, then snap back to the straight-route setting.

serted for example at A and A on opposite sides of the loops.

If you do build a layout like that in Figure 5-4 on shelves, a freestanding table would be needed across the center of the room to support the track near C. Obviously, any of these plans can be built on the floor, in a basement, spare room, or patio, or on a level lawn.

THE "COMPLETE" LGB PLAN

The track plan in Figure 5-5 squeezes a great variety of operation into a space that nearly anyone can find. If you build this layout on a table, it needs to be 6 feet 4 inches wide and 11 feet 8 inches long with only one of the B/B ends against a wall, and aisles along the remaining three sides. This means that, with a bare minimum 18 inches of aisle space, the smallest room this plan could fit would be 9 feet 4 inches wide (6'4" plus twice the minimum 1'6" aisle width) and 13 feet 2 inches long (11'8" plus one 1'6" aisle). Again, it would fit inside one end of a single-car garage and it could be extended to within a couple of feet of the length of the garage by inserting TWO pairs of matching-length straight track sections at the A/A, A/A joints between the track sections.

This plan can be operated in a manner similar to the system just described for the plans in Figures 5-1 and 5-4 except that there is a second, outer, oval. Here, trains begin their journey heading in a counterclockwise direction at number 1. They then travel around most of the outer oval through 2, 3, and 4, to take the straight route through the turnout at 5 to 6 and 7, and into the reversing loop at 8, 9, and 10. The trains are then headed clockwise to reverse their journey from 7 back down to 1.

This plan has an optional pair of turnouts and straight tracks shown in dashed lines near 1. They provide a passing or runaround siding for an extremely short train (perhaps as many as two one-foot cars, if the locomotive is short) so the locomotive can be placed back at the head of the train as described for the out-and-back track in Figure 5-2. The longest route around this layout, then, is for out-and-back operations.

The plan also includes all the two-train operations described for the double-track oval in Figure 5-5. Wiring for the holding track in the outer oval, so that one train can be stopped while the train on the inner oval moves to the outer oval, is not shown. There is also the option, explained in Figure 5-5, of operating one train on a two-lap circuit combining both inner and outer ovals.

The optional track near 1, instead of rejoining the loop, can curve away and extend to various other track arrangements, including any of the yard trackage complexes shown in the LGB Information or the Track Planning books. The track can also be extended into another room or out into the garden to a second reversing loop or a reversing loop and yard.

THE EXPANDABLE LAYOUT

Every track plan in this book is expandable. The bent oval in Figure 5-7, with built-in pairs of reversing loops, lends itself particularly well to expansion by inserting matched pairs of straight track sections at AA and/or BB. Even though the plan is relatively large as compared to the others in this chapter, it is small enough to fit in nearly any spare room or in a corner of the patio or garden.

If the plan is expanded by adding straight track (1000, 1060, or flexible track 1000/5, 1000/3,

Lap Sidings

A lap siding, in which a second siding starts out of the main before the first has re-entered it, allows three

Figure 5-6

trains to meet. Typically, the first two trains take the sidings; the last train uses the main. But as long as the train that takes the main can leave in time to clear the exit siding, any train may take the main. When only two trains meet, the configuration may be operated as two long sidings. Dispatchers love to control this kind of routing.

1000/1) at the points DD and at AA, it can be used to run around any size yard. The major advantage of this plan is that it includes two reversing loops for loop-to-loop operation as described for Figure 5-3, plus a bypass for oval operations. The oval allows the train to run and run in one direction, while the reversing loops provide the ability to turn the entire train without backing up. The wiring is for a simple one-train operation. A layout this large could be

divided with 5026 insulating rail joiners into at least four isolated electrical blocks for running multiple trains (see Chapter 9). Simple wiring is all that is needed, however, if you decide on one of the carrier/command-control systems like Keller's On-board, or PSI's Dynatrol. There is room on this layout, even in the small space shown, to operate at least three trains at once with these sophisticated electronic train control systems.

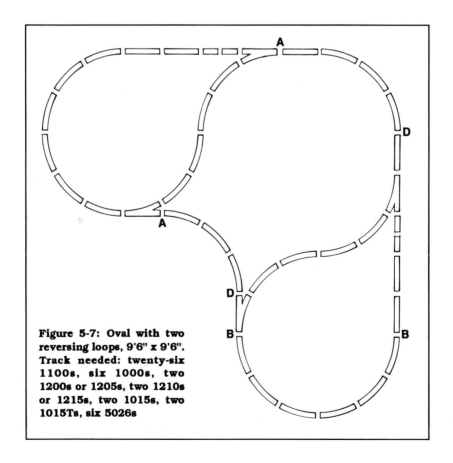

Figure 5-7: Oval with two reversing loops, 9'6" x 9'6". Track needed: twenty-six 1100s, six 1000s, two 1200s or 1205s, two 1210s or 1215s, two 1015s, two 1015Ts, six 5026s

Chapter 6
Preparing Outdoor Layouts

When you build a model railroad outdoors, you are facing many of the same potential problems as the surveyors and engineers building a real railroad. Since you are working with much smaller amounts of dirt and rock and much shorter distances, what is hard work in real life can be a joy and a pleasure in miniature.

To some degree, anyone who builds a model railroad outdoors is fulfilling many of the tasks of a landscape architect. Like these professionals, you must decide what you wish to achieve before you begin work on your garden railroad. There are two options available: build an outdoor model railroad to scale like Robert Treat's and Herb Chaudiere's layouts, or create a garden that happens to include a railroad, like Pete Thorp's and David Charles' layouts. (See Chapter 2, especially "Garden Railway or Outdoor Railroading?")

SURVEYING THE RAILROAD

The simplest way to decide where you want the tracks, for an LGB outdoor layout, is to lay the track where you think you want it. Join a half circle of curved tracks together and use a couple of the 5-foot (1.5 meter) sections of flexible track to help position the straight segments of the layout. You can move a variety of sections around, sketching their locations on a crude drawing of the garden, to determine the approximate placement of the track. Later, you can buy all the track you need or you can start with just a portion of the future layout and expand it as you buy additional track sections.

If you have the space, it is more realistic to use the largest LGB curved track sections (1600), whose

Norm Grant uses a driveway underlay of sand and clay, for ballast, spreading it with a feed scoop.

The ballast is brushed from around the rails and ties with a toothbrush after it has been shaped along the edges.

Right of way construction from right to left: Woven landscaping fabric used as a weed barrier is placed 3 inches or more below the track with 3 inches of medium grit granite paving chips (center) followed by the sand and clay ballast.

nearly four-foot-radius curves double the size of the smallest sections (1100). Most of the outdoor layouts are built with at least a few sweeping curves, even if they are just a few yards long, with an eight-foot radius or larger of track. Though not necessary for layout or for operation, they are cosmetic curves, which add a pleasing appearance. The rails for one of the 5-foot sections of flexible track can be bent to a 8-foot radius using the rail bender tool described in Chapter 3. The smooth curve that results can often be used, in a series of ess-curves, to replace long lengths of straight track.

If the bend is truly gradual, no particular reason for it is needed; but try not to put it right beside a ruler-straight line such as the edge of a flower bed or a lawn: curve them gently, too. The sharper the curve, the more necessary it is to have an explanation for its presence in the surrounding scenery. If you are following an existing curved garden edge, you might want to follow that pattern, as Norm Grant did along the edge of the swimming pool deck on the David Charles' layout.

If you want to swing some large-radius curves, this is the time to get them right. Tie a pencil to the end of a piece of string and drive a surveyor's stake out in the yard or garden where the center of the curve will be; drive a nail in the top of the stake and tie one end of the string to it. Use the string and pencil as a large compass and drive in the surveyor's stakes about every two feet along the projected arc of the curve. Since a curve looks sharpest where it joins a straightaway, try to put a larger radius curve where the curve begins and ends, with a tighter curve in the middle of the arc. The transitional large curves visually serve as easements into and out of the tighter curve, and the whole will look more gradual than a constant radius curve. For now, leave exactly two inches of each stake above what you see as the top of the ground.

DETERMINING GRADE

Although most backyards have at least some kind of slope or pitch, try to keep the top of each stake as level as possible. Use a level by placing it on an 8-foot or longer piece of perfectly straight one-by-four or two-by-four to increase the effective length of the level. The longer board will pass over slight dips or rises to give a truer reading when you measure. The track should not climb more than four inches in one hundred inches of linear travel along the ground. If your backyard slopes more than that BENEATH THE TRACK, you will have to elevate the track on the downhill side to keep it within the four percent grade. The LGB *Moguls* are able to pull about six cars up a four percent grade, but it is a strain. A two percent grade is a better compromise.

Don't worry, for now, if the ground slopes sideways beneath the track; the track can easily be leveled from side to side. Pull the stakes up slightly or push them the remaining two inches into the ground until they are all either level or, if sloping, within the grade range you have chosen.

If the ground drops steeply from beneath the projected railroad, you have several choices:

1. Build a deep fill of dirt and rocks.

2. Build a scale model wood trestle.

3. Build a brick, concrete block, or wooden wall to support the track.

4. Reroute the track to avoid the major change in elevation.

5. Reroute the track (in a series of ess-curves) to make the major change in elevation by a longer and more gradual grade.

THE ROADBED

You will need some type of roadbed beneath the track, if for no other reason than to have some dirt to move around to get the track perfectly level. Since you are going to move dirt in any case, you should consider providing for gully washer rainstorms or overzealous sprinkler use. The drainage you provide, such as a pipe under the track, should keep water from forming puddles or lakes around any turnouts. Also, you can elevate the track to keep it out of the water. Whatever you use must be able to withstand both the constant erosion of rain and wind and the occasional kick by an unwary pedestrian.

Before... The surveyor's stakes were used to mark the right of way, their height adjusted for the proper grade.

...and after. Bender board, from a garden supply, is used to control the edges of the 3-inch layer of granite paving chips. The edge of the concrete pool deck forms one side of this segment of the roadbed.

Nearly every outdoor model railroader feels he has the best solution to the roadbed problem. There is no "best" way. Economy, ease of installation, durability and low maintenance, and ease of relocation cannot all be maximized at once. You can make a sub-roadbed out of creosoted or other treated wood, bricks, tar shingles, tiles of any type, a trough of crushed rock, or even a solid cement river of roadbed that follows the track. You will almost certainly want to relocate the track at some time in the future and that can be difficult, indeed, if the path is literally set in concrete. Some outdoor layouts are even built on six-inch-wide tables elevated a foot or more above the ground to form a type of low shelf. Portions of many outdoor layouts are built on the tops of one or a stack of two or more real railroad ties.

One of the more common methods of building the roadbed for an outdoor layout is to dig a trench at least three inches deep where the track is near the ground. Position one of the garden edging strips such as bender-board or metal corrugations along each side of the trench. The trench should be six inches wide for single track, twice that for sidings, and three times that for three track yards — that is, six inches for each parallel track.

Cut some 4-mil plastic to fill the bottom of the trench. Fill the trench with a material that will drain, like pea gravel or similar-sized granite or other hard rock chips. Keep on filling until there is a pile of

Vertical Curves

A good practice, especially for the steep 4 percent grades but preferable for any grade, is to include at the beginning and end a lesser transitional grade, to make a smooth transition. For example, a 2 percent transition eases the vertical kink where a steep 4 percent grade joins level track. Since a change in grade should be a smooth vertical curve, not an angle, make this whole transitional grade into one smooth curve (use short track sections) and more than one car-length. Note that since it takes a 2 percent grade twice as long as a 4 percent to rise to the same elevation, the transition curves will lengthen the total grade by a minimum of three feet.

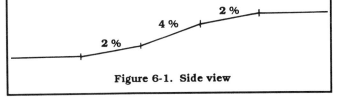

Figure 6-1. Side view

Before...

...and after. Another scene on the David Charles' family layout created for them by Norm Grant. This scene is hidden by bushes so the track is simply laid on top of a creosoted 1:1 scale railroad tie.

chips at least an inch higher than the tops of the stakes that mark the position of the track. If the track is above the ground and fill is required, the fill can be as much as two feet above the ground level but ONLY if you have enough width to let the gravel assume its natural slope on either side. If you lack that room, consider making a solid retaining wall on each side of the track to minimize the width of the fill. Build it like a real wall, with concrete blocks and mortar or firmly set wood posts and well-treated wood walls. With this loose gravel method, it is fairly easy to move the material with a scrap of plywood to make a perfectly level top to support the track. Use the level to check for side-to-side slopes in any areas where three or more tracks are parallel.

LAYING TRACK

A six-inch roadway at the top of the loose pea-sized gravel or chips can then be covered with at least an inch of filler (the sand/clay mix). Be sure that the one-inch layer of filler is perfectly level (side-to-side) and that you have not exceeded your maximum grade. Now, you can place the track on top and press it down so the ties are buried up to within about 1/16 inch of their tops. Use a stiff brush and some gardener's hand tools to work the filler around the track and to shape a ballast edge about a half inch away from the outer ends of the ties. Sweep off all the excess with a stiff four-inch wide paint brush, tighten the rail joiners, and test run some trains.

When you are satisfied with the track location and alignment, check the track for level and grade using a level and a six- or eight-foot board. Add or remove filler from any track sections that sag or bulge. Try to get all this done, of course, before it rains and the clay hardens. After it does harden, you can still alter small areas, without actually ripping the track up, by chopping at any rain-hardened sand and clay with a screwdriver to break it up in place.

As substitutes for the filler, fine gravel or chicken grit can be used. They tend to settle or splash away by rain and therefore require occasional maintenance.

Weed Control

If you are concerned about weeds growing under and around the track, install a weed barrier using black 4-mil plastic or woven landscape fabric. It can be laid on the ground once the track position is marked by stakes and before the roadbed ballast is added. Note: Even if you use some type of weed control, dirt will still accumulate among the ballast material, allowing seedlings to take root. Getting rid of these is part of routine maintenance work.

If at least two inches of roadbed on top of the weed check is desired, determine just which "at grade" level will be the least amount of work. It may be easier to build up or, alternatively, simply to dig a trench three to six inches below the track. If elevating the track, lay the weed barrier right on the ground and build your roadbed up from it about two to six inches. If digging a trench, place the weed stop over the sides and into the trench. Main line and well maintained branch lines on real railroads are always a little higher than the land immediately beside them. Even mountain cuts have drainage ditches on each side. Sidings, yard, and very short, private, industrial, or poorly kept lines may wind up virtually at ground level. Decide which kind of track you are modeling, and how this elevation will relate to rise and fall elsewhere.

Before installation of the wood Howe truss bridge on the concrete blocks used to locate its position...

RAILROADING, RAIN OR SHINE

Just as each season presents a new scene for your models, each season will present a few new problems with your outdoor railroad.

In the spring, you may discover just what the term "washout" means to a real railroad. If a particular area washes away with every rain, consider doing what the real railroads do: fix it. Add a short bridge to let the water flow or perhaps cover the slope with

Or Hire A Pro

If you feel that this type of construction is more than you can handle, and you want something better than you feel you have the skill to build, talk to several landscape architects, landscape gardeners, and even to some contractors who specialize in making sidewalks and driveways. Your problem of wanting a railroad right of way may be unique, but the same solutions that are used to build level outdoor pool decks, shuffleboard courts, or level fences can often be used to build a level and weather-resistant model railroad bed. There are firms that will custom build and landscape your back yard railroad. You may be able to locate one through your local dealer or you might ask your local landscape gardeners if they would create the basic roadbed, at least, for an outdoor layout.

...and after. The concrete blocks were used to locate the position of the wood Howe truss bridge. The blocks are also used as a temporary abutment beneath the ends of the bridge — they will be replaced with more realistic abutments made of redwood strips.

golf ball-sized rocks to control erosion. A short section of three- to six-inch diameter plastic pipe makes a simple culvert. For stability, use the whole cylinder of pipe, burying half of it.

Loose dirt or sand, if close to the track, will spatter onto it during a cloudburst. The solution is a wider gravel roadbed or some kind of ground cover planting. Rain also makes special problems with wood chips, which can float up and away either burying the rails or, if used as ballast, leaving them dangling.

In the summer, the rails will expand and contract as temperatures rise and fall, as the hot sun hits them or cooling dew settles, loosening rail joints.

A dip in the natural slope in David Charles' back yard was spanned with this custom-built Kenosha Railway Supply wood trestle. Note the gradual curves.

Plant growth will be rapid, and unwanted creepers may overflow the track.

Autumn's major problem is falling leaves that cover the track and roadbed and need to be raked off. A hand-held leaf vacuum or blower is a great help in the fall.

Winter will present problems with any trapped water freezing and buckling the roadbed, which is why the porous underlayer of pea gravel or stones is used. Still, you may prevent future problems by replacing the fill with a bridge or a solid chunk of real railroad tie.

All of these are interesting and often enjoyable challenges that make outdoor railroading far more realistic than any other form of model railroading.

Marc Horovitz used a pair of broken drain pipe tiles and some flag stones to make this interesting culvert, whose function is to keep water from accumulating and flowing over the track.

Color Plate 1: Norm Grant has one of the largest outdoor layouts in America. Shown is the LGB 2028D Mogul steaming between moss-covered rocks. Common mint grows above the locomotive, juniper at the left. Norm Grant photo.

Color Plate 2: The rocks on Norm Grant's layout are purchased from a granite quarry; they are "raw" with no moss or lichen. Norm Grant photo.

Color Plate 3: The 4067 LGB boxcar with its late 1800s D&RG lettering waits patiently in the afternoon sun on Norm Grant's western layout. The plantings are a Douglas fir (upper left) and hen-and-chick succulents. Norm Grant photo.

Color Plate 4: Norm Grant transplanted a section of the 4065 LGB caboose body and roof from one end of the cupola to the other to make this rear-cupola caboose, sheathed in Northeastern siding that covers one of the original windows. Norm Grant photo.

Color Plate 5: Norm Grant's train emerges from a real tunnel with a redwood portal. The small-leafed plants are woolly creeping thyme (foreground) and the herb purple sage, above the train. Norm Grant photo.

Color Plate 6: As on the real railroads, bridges must span those places where water will run in a storm. The scene is from Norm Grant's Colorado & Southern. The bridge is hardwood dowels and redwood, the greenery Scotch Pine. Norm Grant photo.

Color Plate 7: A truly spectacular layout: a three-foot high trestle, quarried granite rocks, and timber retaining walls shape the course of Norm Grant's Colorado & Southern. Norm Grant photo.

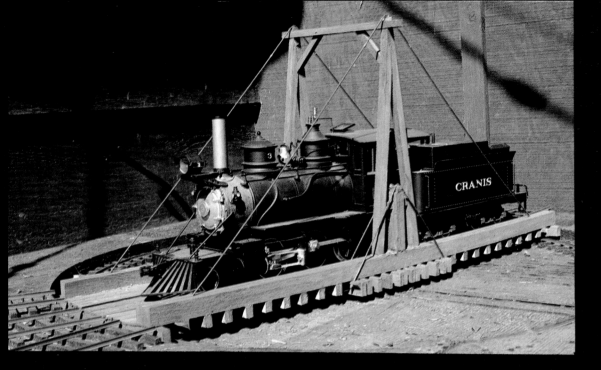

Color Plate 8: On the gallows frame turntable in the terminal at South Eats, Herb Chaudiere's 2-6-0 slowly pivots, to point its MPC headlight, from a 1:24 General kit, back down the track it has just traversed. Herb Chaudiere photo.

Color Plate 9: The Cranis Garden Railway log train squeezes through Mole Hole Pass, as though feeling its way with out-stretched knuckle coupler. Herb Chaudiere photo.

Color Plate 10: A special consist traverses the gentle curve of Bob Johnson's low stripwood trestle on Herb Chaudiere's layout. The small rail, built to 3/8" scale standards that approximate what 1:22.5 narrow gauge standards would be, contributes to the impressive realism of the Cranis Garden Railway. Herb Chaudiere photo.

Color Plate 11: A rocky foreground interrupts the view of Robert Treat's freight, easing cautiously along the precipitous mudbank on his ledge layout. Such visual checks make a train seem longer, a layout larger. Decals and thin paint washes have been added to simulate weathering. Robert Treat photo.

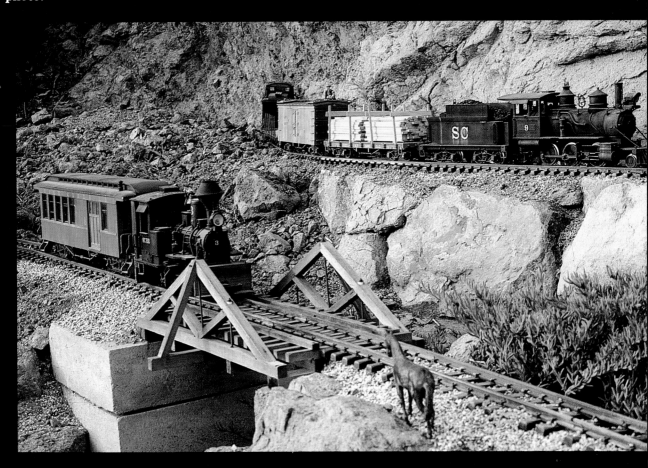

Color Plate 12: A cliff, with a natural 3 foot high bench provided the natural "table" and background cliff for Robert Treat's layout. Robert Treat photo.

Color Plate 13: One of Robert Treat's modified locomotives hauls a small consist (a gondola, converted from a flatcar with strips of wood) through rugged terrain. Robert Treat photo.

Color Plate 14: Neither cold, nor snow, nor piled drifts shall stay the LGB train from its appointed rounds. A scene on the Cranis Garden Railway of Herb Chaudiere.

Color Plate 15: Betty and Earle Thorne routed part of their railroad beneath a 30-foot tall Long Needle pine. Native wild plants, begonias, and moss-covered granite complete the landscape.

Color Plate 16. Trains and flowers interweave dramatically, with harmonizing shapes and colors. Plants, many ordered from Miniature Plant Kingdom, include sub-miniature roses, carnations (Dianthus), Irish and Scotch moss, and Herniaria glabra for ground cover. "Trees" consist of alyssum, verbena, sweet William (Dianthus), lobelia, and candytuft (Iberis). Pete Thorpe photo.

7 (above):   A scene on David Charles' layout.
nd water tower are Pola kits made of a special
plastic. When selecting a building for ground
remember that an interesting roofline can be
as an interesting facade. David Charles photo.

Color Plate 18   (below): The Howe truss bridge was made
by Norm Grant for David Charles using special castings and
threaded rods. The parts and built-up bridges are available
from Kenosha Railway Supply. David Charles photo.

Color Plate 19: An LGB 2018D Mogul crosses a pine trestle made by Norm Grant in David Charles' garden. David Charles photo.

Color Plate 20: The massive 0-6-6-0T articulated 2085 eases through graceful, broad radius curves on David Charles' garden layout. David Charles photo.

Color Plate 22: Gary Nelson's double track right of way defines the boundary between lawn and plantings. He simply cut back the grass area and edged it with a row of bricks between the lawn and the layout. Gary Nelson photo.

Color Plate 23: The plast mountains, made from i dustrial grade paper towe soaked in Hydrocal, ha not yet been colored, b their snowy whitene provides a fantasy bac ground to the sparkling L colors. The model tre maintain a sense of scale their diminutive foliage.

Color Plate 24 (above): Since even the biggest table is small for LGB trains, one solution is to build vertically, as Bill Griffin has done, with elevated tracks, precipitous mountains, and with such sky flyers as balloons.

Color Plate 25 (below): Looming mountains and expansive trestle bridge with an "old-West" station and waiting passengers on this table top layout create a sense of anticipation for the incoming 2018.

Color Plate 26: Large sometimes flat surfaces can be interesting as when mountains are given a rough and mottled texture. The small coal shaft doorway is an eye-catch-

Chapter 7
Landscaping

The term "landscaping" needs a bit of clarification: landscaping is anything you do to the yard to make your model railroad visually more enjoyable for yourself and for your family. Usually, that means making it prettier than just having bare track on bare earth. Just how you beautify the setting of your outdoor railroad depends on what kind of effects you prefer. Landscaping can mean anything from running neatly ballasted track across a lawn as flat and fine as a golf course's putting green to looping track around miniature mountains of dirt and granite. (See Norm Grant's rugged layout on Color Plates 2 and 3.) It can also mean sectional track plopped down on top of a ground cover or an entire miniature world. (See Pete Thorp's flowering kingdom on Color Plate 16.)

Remember, there are diverse garden styles, from alpine gardens with their mossy rocks, to starkly simple Japanese gardens, to gardens of the fleshy green water-storing plants called succulents. You can make any one of these into an accurate scale universe for your model railroad. Or you can make a beautiful garden and simply add the trains as additional decor as you might add a reflecting pool, fountain, or birdbath.

Choices will be easier if you decide on several things in advance. First, is your goal realistic and varied operation, or is it visual effect? That is, will you play the role of engineer or dispatcher, or will you function as spectator? Second, do you want a likeness of the transportation industry, or a beautiful garden? (See "Garden Railway or Outdoor Railroad?" p. 19.) Third, if you want a beautiful garden, will you sacrifice plants for trains, or trains for plants, when they conflict? Fourth, how much of your time will you (or a helper) devote to maintaining right of way? to maintaining plants?

Try to get your priorities clear before you begin your outdoor model railroad. If you are not already

a gardener, the chances are that you won't develop into one just because you have trains running outdoors. It is perfectly permissible to run your trains down a garden sidewalk, whether you create a garden sidewalk to match the path you want your trains to take or lay the track to follow an existing path. It is also possible to add a shelf to a fence around the yard and keep the trains out of the garden and off

Scenes like this require careful planning and positioning of rock and dirt to create natural slopes. Norm Grant's layout uses rocks purchased from a quarry.

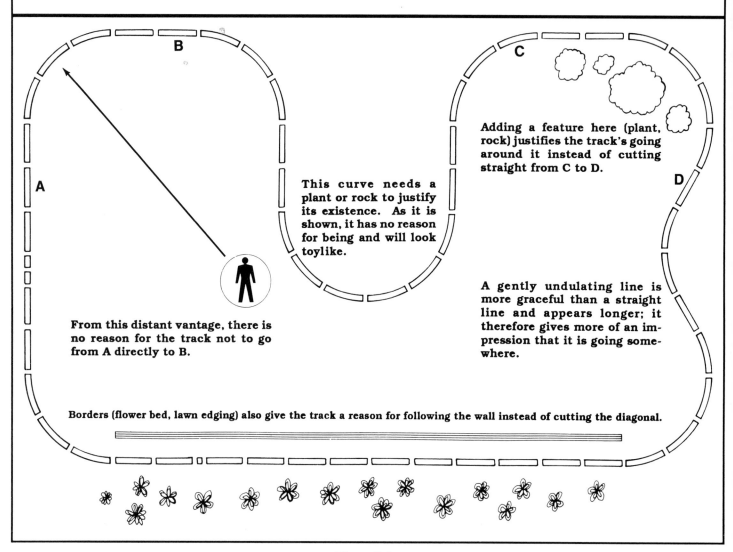

Why Tracks Go Where

Your landscape ought to explain visually why the track goes where it does, whether track or landscape takes precedence in your plan.

B

C

Adding a feature here (plant, rock) justifies the track's going around it instead of cutting straight from C to D.

A

This curve needs a plant or rock to justify its existence. As it is shown, it has no reason for being and will look toylike.

D

A gently undulating line is more graceful than a straight line and appears longer; it therefore gives more of an impression that it is going somewhere.

From this distant vantage, there is no reason for the track not to go from A directly to B.

Borders (flower bed, lawn edging) also give the track a reason for following the wall instead of cutting the diagonal.

Figure 7-1

the lawn completely. Outdoor model railroading and gardening do not have to mix.

You may also decide that you would rather pile rocks than dig in the dirt. If so, build yourself a rock garden or an alpine garden (a rock garden with alpine plants). Robert Treat has created some beautiful settings in nothing but a sandstone cliff (see Color Plates 11 and 12). His railroad right of way provides a pattern through the barren rock similar, in theme, to the Japanese sand gardens. There is no reason, for that matter, why a pattern of model railroad track cannot be incorporated in a Japanese sand garden.

THE ALPINE GARDEN

Most model railroaders prefer to create scenes based on those from real railroads that operated in the mountains. The tight curves and steep slopes make it easier to keep the model railroad within the confines of a spare room or a basement. When you move the railroad outdoors, you expand the available space, but even that backyard has a fence or property line. A mountain railroad is as much a favorite scenic theme for model railroading outdoors as it is indoors.

Before... The piles of granite and flagstone are at the ready to provide a backdrop for the finished track skirting the swimming pool's curved deck.

Outdoors, however, you can use a host of natural materials including real rock ballast and the ultimate, real rocks and boulders for mountains and cliffs. Two of the very best outdoor model railroads with a mountain theme grace the pages of this book: Norm Grant's with its handmade geography and Bob

Treat's with the creative use of a cliff that happened to be hanging over his back yard. (The cliff, by the way, proved to be more of a curse than a blessing. In typical Southern California mud slide fashion, a portion of the cliff sluiced down one rainy night to obliterate half of the original layout. Bob rebuilt it in the form you see in these pages.)

Norm Grant chose to turn his rock garden into an alpine garden. He planned it that way from the start, but the rocks had to come before the plants. He has hauled in 20 tons of rock, and added a few plants. As listed in Chapter 2, they include mostly the hardy and common varieties of herbal sage, mint, phlox, and woolly thyme with trimmed junipers, dwarf Scotch pines, mungo pines, and Douglas firs. He also makes extensive use of moss that is already attached to the rocks and boulders.

GROUND COVER

Ground cover, beyond the ballast, gives a pleasing natural appearance. Grasses are fine as long as you can reach them effectively with a lawn mower or weed cutter. Low-lying plants, like creeping thyme, dicondra, plain clover, Irish or Scotch moss, are all suitable ground covers for different climates around the country.

Within a few months, you may find that the garden is slowly swallowing the railroad. It is not a

...and after. The track in this photograph curves around a large, imposing rock. Notice how the rock, with its resistance emphasized by the overhang, seems to force the train to curve away from it. Here, the scenery and track layout work together.

good idea, for example, simply to lay tracks right on a lawn even if the lawn happens to be your own private putting green. It only takes an inch or two of growth for the blades of grass to lie across the rails and bring both the Overnight Limited and the Oak Tree Local to a stuttering halt. Pure sand or rock ballast, however, will NOT prevent the lawn or weeds from covering the track and stopping operation; in fact, most weeds will grow even faster in the ballast. Some type of barrier, like 4 mil thick black plastic sheeting, is needed between the soil and the ballast. You can bury bricks or real railroad ties, or drop the ties or bricks on the lawn or dirt and put the track on top of them. The lesson, here, is that you want to landcape ONLY up to the edges of the ballast.

GARDEN RAILROADING EXPERTS

You may be an expert railroader; what you may need is an expert gardener. Start at the local nursery and find out from them what type of ground covers and miniature shrubs and trees require the least effort to survive in your particular part of the country. If you don't get the answers you want, try the nearest college that offers horticultural courses. Most colleges have some type of consulting services. A third alternative is the horticultural department of your local county extension office. If you live in an urban area, try a more rural adjacent county. All of these specialists know what will grow best in your area. Be sure the experts you select understand the alkalinity or acidity of your soil and whether the plants you choose will be grown in direct sunlight or in partial shade from surrounding full-sized trees, fences, or structures.

All you need from your local experts is the names of the plants that have a size, shape, and color that pleases you. Your local nursery can probably supply the plants or you may be able to order a starter plant in a small pot from a mail order nursery. Again, ask the local experts. Or write a plant supplier, such as Dan Herzog at the Miniature Plant Kingdom (see

Mrs. David Charles planted part of her miniature alpine garden before the track was in place, but the trees and ties were placed to clear the proposed track route. Notice that the bush and rock require the train to snake between them in an ess-curve which is made to appear as gradual as possible.

Appendix: Supply Sources). Plant catalogues can list hundreds of varieties, but may not be illustrated, so you will need to know the names of suitable plants.

If you are going to build a model railroad the size of LGB, you really should subscribe to *Garden Railways* magazine (see Appendix: Publications.) The bimonthly publication averages about 32 pages and includes a color cover and, often, color photos. Every issue has at least one article on how to create a realistic landscape for your model railroad. Past issues have included excellent articles on alpine gardening and on topics such as how to keep Trident Maple, Japanese Grey-bark Elm, Hollywood Juniper, and Cottoneaster trees smaller than two feet at full maturity.

MINIATURE FORESTS

The obvious solution to the problem of finding scale-sized trees is to use Bonsai tree species and techniques. That, however, is a hobby unto itself that may or may not enhance your enjoyment of outdoor model railroading. There are several alternatives, including careful selection of dwarf bushes that can be pruned and trimmed to look like scale model trees. Start your search in the hills and forests near your home; you may be able to find some natural bushes, like small sage, that can be transplanted to thrive on a small scale in your back yard.

Look in a Book

Your local library or nursery should have a variety of books that can be helpful for your particular soil and climate conditions. Check your library's index under these headings:

"Miniature Plants"

"Gardening, Miniature" and

"Gardening, Rock"

to find titles that include plants you can grow successfully for your garden railroad.

If you are going to purchase small plants, consider the varieties of Japanese maple like *acer palmatum*, and varieties of Japanese False Cypress like *Chamaecy paris pisifera Nana* to simulate deciduous trees. Try the *Juniperus communis Compressa* for scale-sized junipers, Norway Spruce, including *Picea abies Little Gem*, or one of the varieties of American *arbor vitae* like *Thuja accidentallis recurva Nana*. Your local expert should be able to tell you if any of these can grow in your back yard or suggest a substitute of similar appearance.

SCALE TREES AND SHRUBS

One of the goals of many model railroaders is to duplicate every aspect of the real world to a precise scale. That scale reduction carries right through, from the overall size of the locomotives, down to the proper height rail, and even to the size and texture of the ballast granules. However, precise scale is nearly impossible to accomplish with LGB equipment outdoors. Robert Treat's layout, although it had no plants on his sandstone cliff, is perhaps the closest to scale among those in this book. Herb Chaudiere has the scale track work but he has been willing, so far, to settle for out-of-scale plants.

As discussed earlier, LGB is a stand-off scale, where the models are designed to be viewed from more than about three feet. The plants and foliage used with this equipment generally fall into that category. Yes, it is possible to find nearly scale leaves, but any coniferous plants will have needles that are way out of scale. Remember, at 1:22.5 scale a three-inch-long leaf will be only 1/8 inch long. You

Norm Grant used one-by-six redwood boards to make the sides and roof of this tunnel. A Kenosha Railway Supply wood tunnel portal will be added later.

can find such plants, but creating an entire garden with scale as an absolute criterion for plant selection is going to require a great deal of work.

It can probably be done. There are layouts to 1/12 scale, and some garden cities in European parks that have scale-sized foliage. But most American garden railroaders are perfectly willing to utilize the vast variety of plants that have small leaves and small overall sizes. If you keep the overall height of any trees to less than three feet, the effect is very pleasing. A three-foot high tree would be the equivalent in scale of an average-sized (seventy foot high) tree to an LGB-sized man.

Chapter 8
Indoor Layouts

One of the endearing characteristics of real railroads is that they are so very, very big. It is difficult to capture that feeling of massive power with a train that is no bigger around than your thumb. LGB-sized models, in contrast, have the mass you expect from a real railroad train. Their size is even more apparent when you operate them indoors where they can be viewed up close and, if you wish, from a track side vantage point, either by lying down on the floor where they are, or by raising them up on table work at eye-level.

Indoor/outdoor carpeting can be used to insulate the layout from the dust and dirt of a concrete basement or patio floor.

FINDING SPACE
FOR AN INDOOR RAILROAD

If you're a newcomer to the hobby of model railroading, you should know right off about the modeler's universal dilemma: there is never enough

space for the railroad you want to build. There is seldom enough space even when you build a layout outdoors. The dream is to have just one more small town, or another trestle, or another 30-foot run of sweeping ess curves, on and on and on.... Do understand, though, that you can build a delightful model railroad indoors even with equipment as large as LGB's.

The prototypes that LGB selected for all their models are narrow gauge locomotives and rolling stock, replicas of quaint little pieces of equipment that, somehow, seem to be even more charming in models this size. The real equipment was designed for the same reason LGB selected it as their prototype: its ability to negotiate sharp curves. The real railroads needed hairpin curves to avoid expensive cuts, fills, tunnels, and bridges; the surveyors and engineers simply skirted the hills and mountains following the natural contour lines.

For the modeler, LGB track can be fitted in as small a linear space as HO scale models. How, when LGB is at least four times the size of HO? By utilizing its narrow gauge locomotives, cars, and track work. A 24-inch radius curve has long been regarded as standard on HO layouts; that is the radius of the smallest LGB curve (for which there is at least one prototype: a hairpin turn on the Darjeeling and Himalayan).

The common European prototype foot-long, two-axle LGB cars (such as the 4030 boxcar) are virtually the same length as a modern 80-scale-foot HO car. The diminutive six-inch LGB cars, such as the 4047 wine car and 4045 bulkhead flatcar with stakes, suitable for American industrial and plantation railroads, are close to the length of a 40-scale-foot HO car.

The turnouts branch more gradually. LGB's 1200s need two linear feet to branch to parallel track; HO's "standard" no. 6 turnouts need a little over a

Unusual Solutions

Some modelers make surprising compromises with standard practices, with happy results. George Nachwalter has an operating layout high on the wall of his entry hall: it is 8 x 84, in inches, not feet. A single line of track lies in front of beautifully modeled relief flats, and a trolley car runs back and forth, automatically reversing. The appeal is the visual charm of the animated scene.

For longer gallops, he has four lines in his one-car garage. The entry door is in one short wall, the auto door in the other. The lowest line is an oval, on a table against a long wall, with a stub branch running past the auto door and down the other long wall, the aisle way between. The second level is a U of track, from long wall to long wall via the auto door. The third level is an oval around the four walls, with a swing-aside bridge section at the pedestrian door. The fourth level, still incomplete, runs along one long wall. None of the four levels has any connection to any of the others. The appeal again is largely visual with the spaces crowded with scratch-built buildings detailed down to discarded beer cans, and items from Simone Nachwalter's miniature collection.

At Carter Colwell's house, the recently dismantled Electric Cadman and Colville Railway Company ran along the walls, from a loop in the rear bedroom, through the hall, around the carpeted living room under sofas and tables and behind chairs and desk, through a hole in the wall under the stairs, through the guest closet to a loop in the guest front bedroom. Hallway door bottoms were trimmed slightly so they could close over the track; the guest double bed was raised two and a half feet, anchored to the wall at the head for stability and held by two vertical pipes at the foot, to allow clear view of buildings inside the reversing loop beneath the bed. Two or three pieces of balsa stripwood, cut to length, were fitted inside the hollow tie-bottoms of each piece of LGB track, with a single drop of rubber cement to hold them in place. When the track was positioned, the wood was glued to the terrazzo floor, holding the track in position even when stubbed by strangers' toes. The track could be lifted from the balsa for dusting.

foot, a difference related to track width. Barely two parallel tracks of LGB will fit into a foot-wide space, whereas six HO will fit. Except for a main line, LGB's narrow gauge G scale requires little more space than standard gauge HO.

To get mountain grades on his floor layout, this operator used one-by-fours and 1/2 inch plywood to make the vertical risers to elevate his track. The roadbed was cut to fit the track from 1/2 inch plywood.

FLOOR LAYOUTS

The rugged construction of LGB track offers you an option that is not really practical with the flimsier HO or N scale track: you can lay LGB track right on the floor or carpet. (But try not to step on track that lies on soft carpet.) With the LGB number 1150 Track Clips, you can temporarily lock as many as a dozen pieces of track together into sections as large as 4 x 4 feet. When it is time to lift the trackage to clear the room for other activities or to vacuum the carpet, you may only need to pull apart a dozen track joints. The large modules of track sections can then be stored upright against the wall. You can even use this semi-portable system on a two-car garage floor, if you don't mind carrying oil stains back to the track storage area. All but one of the track plans in Chapter 2 can be fitted into a 10 x 12-foot room. To fill a one- or two-car garage, they may be expanded.

TABLE TOP LAYOUTS

The ideal location for an indoor model railroad is, of course, a table designed expressly for the layout. A model railroader often builds the table as a grid-work of one-by-four boards on edge with an additional one-by-four spaced about every two feet across any open areas. This type of construction is called *open grid.*

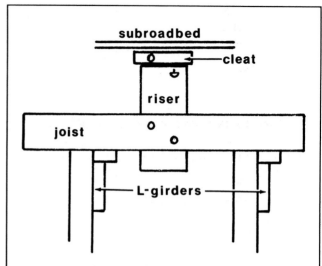

Figure 8-1: To make an L-girder, clamp one-by-two atop one-by-four; screw (1-1/4 inch #8 flathead) every foot (pilot holes make it easier); remove screws; apply white glue (such as Elmer's) to joint; reassemble with screws and let dry for 24 hours. Screws then may be removed or left in place.

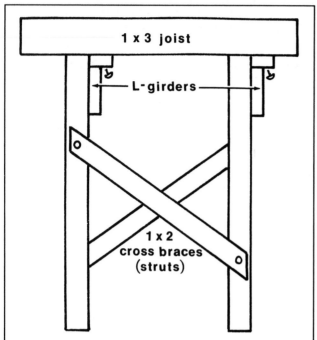

Figure 8-2: Assemble two pairs of legs with diagonal struts, one screw per joint; clamp to L-girder (flanges forward), level girders; screw girders to legs; trim off leg tops; install two joists, one at each pair of legs, driving screws up through lip of a one-by-two flange.

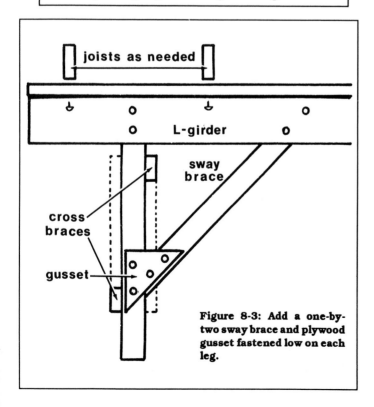

Figure 8-3: Add a one-by-two sway brace and plywood gusset fastened low on each leg.

Figure 8-4: Support plywood subroadbed with one-by-four risers, clamped to joists, leveled, and then screwed in place. Do not screw roadbed directly to riser: use a cleat instead (see Figure 8-5). Note that since joist overhangs girder, it can be trimmed to make a narrow waist where needed, and a curving fascia of 1/8 inch fiberboard, cut along the top to match hill elevation contour, can be mounted on the joist ends.

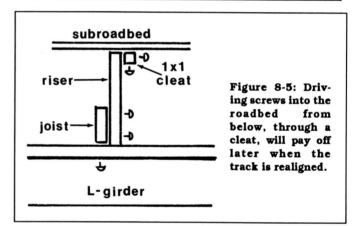

Figure 8-5: Driving screws into the roadbed from below, through a cleat, will pay off later when the track is realigned.

Kalmbach Publishing Company (see Appendix: Publications) also sells a book explaining the open grid method. The basic idea is twofold:

1) An L-shaped wooden girder provides efficient longitudinal strength.

2) Elevated roadbed, raised on vertical risers above horizontal joists which sit across the tops of a pair of L-girders, both provides easy adjustment of grade or track location because all screws are driven from below, and also makes wiring easy to reach.

The system is strong and economizes on material. Two pairs of two-by-two legs, braced in both directions, will support a pair of 20-foot-long girders.

After framework is constructed, the track work is then planned full size and traced on sheets of plywood. The plywood is cut about an inch wider than the outside of the ties to provide a roadbed. The areas where there are no tracks are left open to be covered by plaster scenery, often below the track level. However, plywood bases are cut to cover the open grid areas wherever buildings or towns are to be located, to give a flat site. Most modelers also elevate all of the plywood on vertical risers, a standard feature of L-girder construction to raise the tracks far enough above the open gridwork of the table to leave room below them for valleys and rivers. Easier wiring is another benefit.

A note about **plywood vs. particle board**. Plywood is more expensive than particle board, but it has several advantages and is strongly recommended. Plywood is sturdier, easier to work with, provides a quieter base, and is flexible. The last is an important attribute when constructing a model railroad. Particle board, on the other hand, cracks if dropped, breaks off easily, and is very heavy compared to plywood. In addition, it reverberates loudly when trains run over it and it is not water resistant.

It is certainly possible to build an LGB layout on a flat table top as small as 5 x 9 feet. Some lumber dealers carry plywood in that size to be used for ping pong tables. When you are building a table top layout, however, remember that you must be able to reach ALL the track work for maintenance and to rerail the equipment if it does fall off the track. Two and a half feet is about the maximum distance you can reach comfortably and effectively, which means you could NOT reach the back of a 5 x 9 foot table if you placed the 9 foot edge against the wall (see Figures 8-6 and 7). If you do use a 5 x 9 foot table, the 5-foot end is the only one which can be placed against the wall (see Figure 8-8). This creates a peninsula layout that allows you to walk around three sides only. If you can place the table in the

Bob Leners used open grid bench work made of one-by-four boards for his S scale (3/16 inch to the foot) indoor layout. A layer of Homosote, cut to shape, lies between the track and roadbed. The same system will work nicely with LGB.

middle of the room it becomes what modelers call an "island layout," one that can be operated or viewed from all four sides.

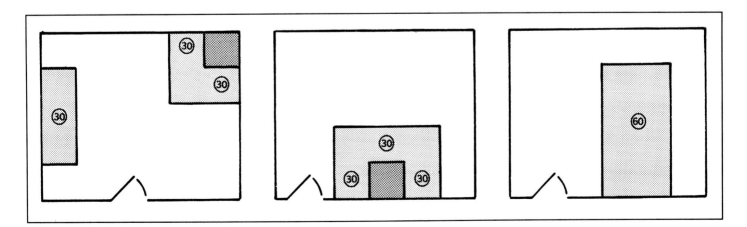

Figure 8-6: A corner layout bigger than normal reach (30 inches) in its smaller dimension will have inaccessible areas (shaded). Figures 8-7 and 8-8: A peninsula layout can be any length as long as the side along the wall is no more than twice normal reach (2 x 30 inches, or five feet).

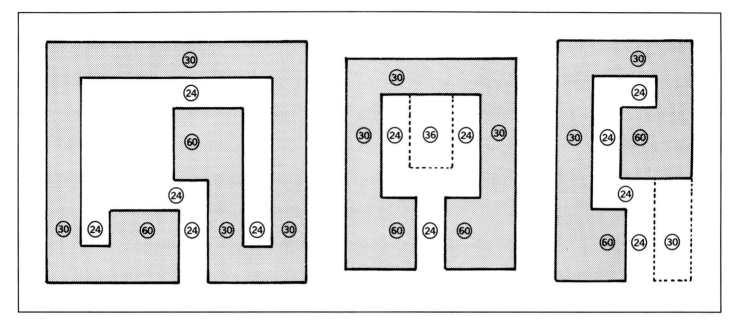

Figures 8-9, 8-10, and 8-11: Table plans for loop-to-loop around-the-wall shelf and peninsula layouts, with no-stoop entry, using 30-inch shelves, 24-inch aisles, and 60-inch squares for reversing loops. Shelves can be narrow-waisted at critical points for some reduction. Notice that a long peninsula extension without turnaround might be added in the middle of 8-10, and a similar extension beside the door in 8-11.

ISLAND VS. SHELF-STYLE LAYOUTS

Island or peninsula layouts waste some of the room space, as compared to layouts located on shelves around the walls of the room. All of the plans in Chapter 2, though, are designed for island or peninsula layouts. Remember that you need 18-inch-wide aisles along at least three sides. Two feet is more comfortable, but at least two and a half feet is desirable if more than one person is to use the aisle at a time.

When you put the layout on shelves around the room, a center access area is used and, in most rooms, that center area wastes less space, leaving more square feet for the model railroad. The appearance of the trains improves, too, when seen from the inside of curves. (Spaces between cars are oversized in the models, and from the outside of a curve the gap widens and looks even less realistic.)

The problems with shelf layouts that have continuous running (there are no design problems with point-to-point layouts) are doorways through layouts that circle the room, and locating the healthy chunk of real estate needed for reversing loops in layouts that run loop-to-loop.

Doorway problems can be solved with *duck-unders* which some people find uncomfortable to use; drop leaves which are dangerous to trains unless you *interlock* the track circuit with the leaf so that a train can't run onto an unfastened drop leaf; and lift-up sections which are harder to hinge than the drop leaf, because the track sticks up above the table (these

are also somewhat dangerous unless track current is interlocked, because of the danger of running into a void). The 1009 adjustable track section eases some of the track connection problems with drop leaves and lift-outs.

Reversing loop location problems disappear if the room is as large as 18-1/2 x 17 feet, the size of most two-car garages; by narrowing the shelves at crucial areas, one of the dimensions may be less. The loops can then sit beside one another in the center, with space left for aisle ways. (See Figures 8-9, 10, 11)

Remember that shelves cannot be any wider than 30 inches, if you are to reach the back edges for painting and detailing. Although shelf-style layouts with LGB equipment are rare, they are the favorites of experienced model railroaders in the smaller scales. The shelf itself is either anchored to the wall or is a free-standing table that just happens to circle the room. Again, open grid and L-girder constructions are easier to scenic than a flat table top.

If you are going to build an indoor layout on a table top or shelf, at least consider making the table chest-high rather than the conventional thirty-inch table height. The models look much more like the real thing when they are viewed from this angle. Outdoors, you have natural lighting and scenery to create the illusion of reality-reduced-to-miniature. Indoors, you need to use some other tricks including a more realistic viewing angle.

Alternatively, consider keeping a couple of free-wheeling chairs on rollers in the railroad room, one for you and one for a guest. Sitting down to operate lowers your viewpoint, with the same increase in realism as raising the layout height. When you do stand up to work on the layout, the fact that you can bend over the lower layout will increase your reach. For working on a high layout, a stool is handy.

Also, if you're building a shelf-style layout, cover the walls of the room with wallboard or linoleum between the tops of the tables and the ceiling. Curve the boards around each corner and spackle-in any seams. To give the layout room the illusion of being outdoors, paint the boards sky blue, which results in a much paler color than you may think.

INDOOR RIGHT OF WAY

If you are building a layout on a table top, support the track work with plywood that is at least 1/2 inch thick. If you are elevating the roadbed above the open grid, place the vertical supports no farther than 24 inches apart beneath the plywood so the plywood cannot sag. You can nail the plywood directly to the riser, but only if you know you will never want to move it. A screw driven through a cleat from below (the cleat in turn screwed to the riser, as in L-girder construction) allows you to change your mind in a year or two and move track easily. Track can be tacked lightly in place with short nails, whose heads will not go through the holes provided in ties near the end of each section. The nail should fit easily in the hole without friction and not be hammered down tightly, which could change the gauge slightly.

The trains will be very noisy with the plywood acting a bit like a drumhead to increase the effect of the noise. Model railroaders often cover the plywood with a layer of 1/2 inch Homosote or 1/4 inch Upsom board. These are almost identical to gray cardboard, but much thicker. Your local lumberyard may be able to order either Homosote or Upsom board in 4 x 8-foot or larger sheets. These materials are strong enough to hold the nails that position the track, but soft enough to absorb sound. Cut the boards with a saber saw (using a knife-style blade or a saw blade with coarse teeth to avoid clogging the blade) just an inch wider — 1/2 inch on each side — than the ends of the ties. The boards will make it easier to fill in around the track with ballast.

Model railroaders have developed some techniques that make it easier to ballast the track. You should be able to obtain crushed rock with a granule fine enough to be used for ballast on your LGB track. Model railroad shops sell bags of ballast, but it is too small for LGB equipment. A good substitute is kitty litter or chicken grit. Spread the ballast over the track and shape the edges to match those on real railroad track. Brush any granules away from the

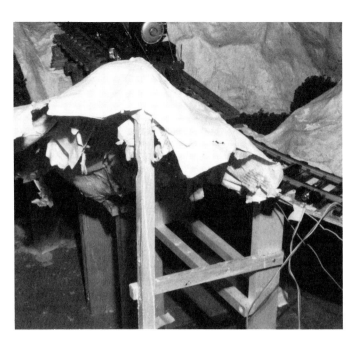

The roadbed supports the bottom of the mountains with two-by-two boards beneath the peaks. The shapes are Hydrocal plaster-soaked industrial paper towels.

turnouts. Apply some LaBelle number 106 oil to all the working and sliding portions of the points at each turnout so you won't glue them shut. Finally, soak the entire track and ballast, EXCEPT WHERE THE TURNOUT POINTS MOVE, with a mixture of equal parts water and artists' matte medium, with a few drops of liquid detergent in each quart. The matte medium dries clear and flat while the detergent helps to break the water's surface tension so it will soak through the ballast. Literally flood the area again, except around the turnout points, so it all looks milky white. When it dries, the ballast will be held firm but with a relatively soft bond that does not transmit noise as much as if you used plain white glue. The matte medium is also slightly flexible, so it is easier to pry up the track if you want to relocate it later.

OUTDOOR SCENERY INDOORS

Once again, model railroaders have developed indoor scenery construction techniques that are relatively easy to use and almost as effective as the real thing. One modeler used the basic mountain making techniques on his indoor LGB layout shown above and in Chapter 2. A simple grid of vertical boards is constructed to support only the peaks and ridges of the mountains. He used two-by-twos; since the plaster (Hydrocal) once dry is self-supporting, lighter lumber, down to one-by-one, will serve for shorter vertical supports if attached to a sturdy framework such as L-girder table work. Ridges for mountains can be roughly shaped by crumpled up dry newspaper supported either by the table surface or by a light mesh of masking tape or cardboard strips, strung from post to post as needed. (An alternative material to use on the formwork is fiberglass windowscreen.) Get all the mountain shapes just the way you want them with the damp newspapers, but don't fret; changes can be made easily, overlaying or replacing unwanted shapes.

Mask the track carefully with drafting tape, which doesn't leave as much of a sticky residue as masking tape. To make mountains, layers of newspapers, dampened with a plant sprayer so they are flexible, are then draped over the posts and stapled to the edges of the plywood roadbed, leaving the top of the wood free so the plaster can bond to it.

The actual scenery surface will be made from Hydrocal plaster. Hydrocal, so named because as the water (hydro) dries out the plaster warms (cal) up, is a very hard plaster, almost an alabaster, that is used for casting statues and for industrial plaster work. Large lumberyards carry it or can order it in 100-pound bags.

Mix about two pounds of Hydrocal at a time, slowly pouring it into a flexible and easy to clean plastic dishpan, stirring to mix out any bubbles or lumps. Use enough water to make the mixture the consistency of thick cream. If you can, buy some industrial grade brown paper towels from a janitorial

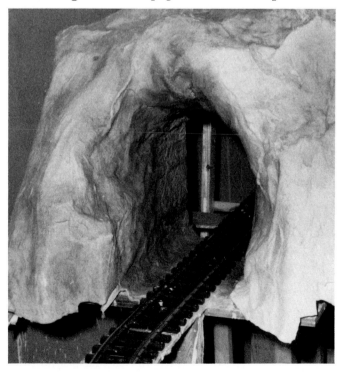

The inside surfaces of the tunnels on this basement layout were formed before the mountains were added. Foil-wrapped tubes were used to shape the tunnels.

The mountain shapes on Bob Leners' S scale narrow gauge layout are made of corrugated cardboard strips (masking tape can be used) supported by two-by-two vertical posts. The rocks are available as plaster castings from hobby dealers.

supply firm; otherwise, use the strongest paper towels your local grocery store sells. Dip one of the paper towels at a time into the Hydrocal mix and drape the wet towel over the newspaper-shaped mountains. Repeat the process until the entire scenery area is covered, right up to the edges of the plywood, with two layers of the Hydrocal-soaked paper towels.

You will, of course, need to make many batches of Hydrocal, but two pounds is about all you can use at a time before the material begins to harden. One modeler removed his track before applying the Hydrocal so he could cover the roadbed with the plaster-soaked towels. This saves a lot of masking but it will increase operating noise.

You can bind the first layer of the Hydrocal-soaked paper towels to the edges of the plywood roadbed beside the masked track by stapling the towels to the plywood with a staple gun. Insert the staples within five minutes or less after you've applied the Hydrocal, while it is hardening but before it has time to set.

The Hydrocal can be precolored with the powders used to color concrete driveways. Mix the colored powder into the water just before you begin to pour in the Hydrocal powder. A good mixture is dark brown (burnt sienna) and black. This technique can save a lot of paint and, if the plaster does chip or if you miss a spot with the paint, it will show brown rather than glaring white. Some modelers use a finer plaster finish coat such as Plaster of Paris, on top of the Hydrocal, finishing a small area at a time, to work in more detailed rock formations with a knife and spatula edge.

You can paint the mountains with latex wall paint, but have several cans of *ground foam* and sifted dirt ready to sprinkle on the still wet paint to create a textured surface. Hobby shops sell ground foam from firms like Woodland Scenics, Life-Like, and AMSI; or use dried coffee grounds from the kitchen or dirt from your back yard, sifting the dirt through a tea strainer screen to cull the larger rocks and pebbles. These leftover rocks and pebbles can be used for special areas like the edges of rivers or streams.

Even if you don't paint, the Hydrocal can be "zip-textured" by wetting it with a sprayer and sifting a mixture of dry Hydrocal and plasterer's dry colors

This modeler made the supports for the bridges before covering the supports with plaster. He removed the track so the plaster-soaked paper towels could be laid right over the roadbed.

(browns, yellows, greens, earth reds, black, according to whether your mountains represent dry sierras or lush alpine areas). The mixture should represent earth and ground-covering plants, not rock; it will naturally fall and drip onto the horizontal ledges where dirt and grass grow, and give a very realistic effect quickly and easily.

INDOOR PLANT LIFE

It is easier to create more realistic foliage for an LGB layout indoors than outdoors. Outdoors, it is almost impossible to grow plants with 1:22.5 scale leaves or pine needles. Indoors, ground foam produces what appear to be perfect scale leaves. Hobby stores also carry a variety of flocking powders from Heki, Sommerfelt, and Vintage Reproductions. Dealers can order them from Walthers. The individual flocking strands are almost perfect LGB-scale pine needles or individual blades of grass. Ready-made trees are available from Life-Like and Heki.

Natural materials for trunk and branch structures can be used to make realistic trees; small hedge clippings, wild sagebrush limbs, and other scale-sized branching structures can be flocked with leaf material to make deciduous trees. Bend the Heki and Life-Like ready-made conifers and spray them with some slightly lighter colors, for highlights, to increase their realism.

Chapter 9
Electrical Wiring

LGB uses a two-rail system of carrying the electrical current to and from the locomotive's motor that is both simple and practical. The basic system is the same used for HO scale model trains, except that at top speed LGB requires 18 volts DC (direct current), while most HO scale models require 12 volts DC. Also, while most HO locomotives have a metal frame, LGB locomotives have a plastic frame. Interior power wiring consists of shaped and bent brass strips, each serving as an electrical bus. One rail carries the current to the locomotive's driving wheels and, in many cases, a sliding contact. They, in turn, carry it through metal brushes and springs to the brass conductor strip that leads to the motor. The current is returned through a mirror route on the other side, ending where wheels ride on rail.

Simple or Complex?

The amount of wiring you must do and how complex it will be depends on several factors:

1. What kind of train control you use.
2. How many engines will either sit or run on the layout at one time.
3. How many train-turning units (reversing loops, wyes, turntables) you have.
4. How much automatic control you want.
5. How many electrical accessories (lights, signals, electric crossing gates, etc.) you have.

A variety of firms offer power packs that include a transformer (to transform the household voltage of 110 volts to a much less harmful 18 volts), a rectifier (to rectify household alternating current to direct current), a throttle (speed controller), and a switch to reverse direction. LGB offers 5000, 5003, and 5006 transformers. The 5000 and 5003 have throttles and reversing switches. The 5006 is just the power portion of a power pack; it is meant to be used with separate 5007 or 5012N throttle/reversing controls. The use of the separate throttle allows the 115-volt transformer/rectifier to be located indoors out of the weather, with the low-powered 18-volt throttle located nearer the track, outdoors if necessary. Various other firms (Polks/Aristo Craft, Starr, and Model Rectifier) also make transformer/rectifiers that deliver 18 volts DC with enough current capacity for the larger LGB motors and two-motor locomotives. The throttles are built into the power packs sold by these firms.

The 5016/1 LGB track connecting terminals must be assembled and snapped around the base of the rail as shown, and of course a wire must be attached. 5016 comes ready to use, with the wire leads attached to the track clips.

The 1015K reversing loop set includes the 1015K diode-equipped track (bottom) and a 1015T section with gaps in both rails.

TRACK WIRING

Outdoor Considerations: None of the transformer/rectifiers are designed to be used outdoors. You can, however, leave the LGB 5007 and 5012 throttles in the yard. Your wiring will, of course, have to withstand the rigors of weather. The wires can lie on the ground, but it is neater to bury them. All-weather insulated 14 gauge household wiring cables are fine for use outside. The wires can be buried by digging a simple slit in the ground and inserting the wire, then pushing the sides of the slit back together. Some modelers, however, bury lengths of the metal or plastic tubing used to run wires in industrial applications. The loose wires are then run through the tubes. This method has the advantage of allowing you to pull one of the wires out to replace it; and there is less chance of accidentally shearing the wire if someone happens to dig or shovel in just the wrong place.

Oxidation is the bane of outdoor electric trains. When brass rail oxidizes, it forms an insulating coat that weakens the flow of electric current and may stop it completely. The inside of the rail joiner will eventually oxidize, too. For this reason, the five-foot 1005/5 rails are preferable to the two-foot 1060 rail sections: there are fewer rail joints.

In addition, jumper wires, soldered in an omega shape (or a U with big serifs) around the rail joint, pay long-term dividends. Make *jumper wires* of stranded, flexible wire, with enough slack to let you pull the rail joint apart and refasten it. Prototype rail

often has such jumper wires to carry signals past the rail joints.

Do not use acid-core solder or acid flux when soldering electrical joints; the acid will eventually corrode the joint enough to destroy electrical contact, even though the connection looks sound. Use resin flux or solders sold specifically for electrical use. To prevent electrical connections from oxidizing, coat the wire terminals and plugs with a light layer of dielectric grease, available at larger automotive parts stores.

An alternative approach is to screw terminals to each side of the joint using a small machine screw (you will have to drill and tap a hole in the track and solder the wire to the terminals). This saves heating up the rail and possibly damaging the plastic ties.

On a large outdoor layout, the most remote track can be a long way from the supply. Use extra feeder wires in the same track circuit, to compensate for voltage loss as the current makes its way through the track.

LGB books include a variety of ways to use the 1015U section with one insulated rail and a diode when throwing turnouts automatically to start and stop trains.

Indoor Wiring: Run wires below the bench work or table top. Always put at least one pair of right-angle bends in a wire route, so you have slack and can move it out of the way when adjusting bench work, track, or scenery. Fancy ties are available for grouping wires into neat cables, but the twist-ties for plastic bread or garbage bags work as well. A smaller

Wiring: Track and Power

Electrical operation has two components:

1. Wiring the track. It is essentially a matter of maintaining good contact and preventing short circuits, at switches and turning tracks.

2. Distributing the power. It is a question of train control: getting different locomotives to do different things simultaneously.

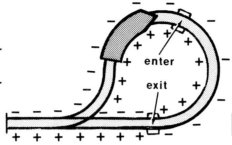

Figure 9-1: Why a reversing loop needs an insulated track section. When the track curves around to re-join itself, what was the inner rail now connects to the outer rail, and vice versa.

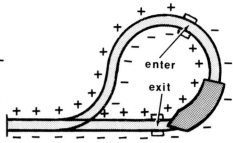

Figure 9-2: This reversing loop's insulated track section is set for the train to enter from the top side. However, if the train tries to exit, there will be a short circuit at the bottom. Even a motorless car will make a short circuit there, if it has metal wheels.

Figure 9-3: The insulated track section keeps its polarity; but the main line, including the turnout, has been reversed by the operator. The train, already in the isolated section, now can exit forward onto the main line, without causing a short circuit.

gauge of wire (the bigger the number, the thinner the wire and therefore the smaller its gauge) usually suffices for the shorter lengths of wire typical of indoor layouts; 18 gauge wire should be adequate for a layout in a single room, with smaller gauges (20 or 22) suitable for short connections.

Turning tracks — Reversing loops: One of the few problems with the two-rail system of providing electric current is the turning track. When the track turns back upon itself to form a reversing loop, like the profile of a teardrop (see Chapter 5), the left rail going into the loop curves around to join what was the right rail going into the loop (and vice-versa). The result is a short circuit, since the left and right rails have opposite polarity.

An electrically isolated segment of track, with both rails insulated at each end, must be installed so that the plus/minus polarity of the main line can be reversed with a separate control switch (a double pole, double throw electrical switch —DPDT—wired as a reversing switch) while the locomotive completes its reversing path through the isolated block of track. While the train is in the isolated block, the power direction on the main line is reversed.

The isolated track must be at least as long as the distance from the train's front metal wheel, probably on its engine, to its last metal wheel, possibly on its caboose. Note, too, that the operator manually reverses the main line direction, but it is possible to arrange for this to happen automatically. .

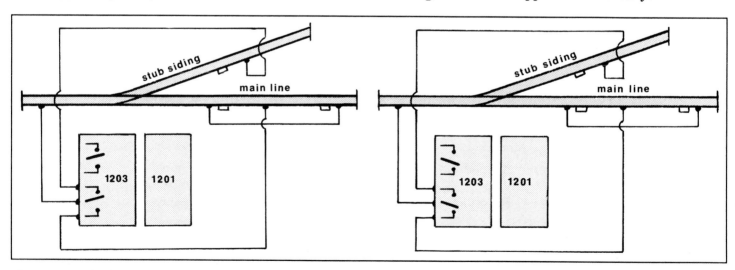

Figures 9-4 and 9-5: A slave to 1201, 1203 on the left (Figure 9-4) is set to feed current to the stub; on the right (Figure 9-5) is set to feed current to the main. Throwing the 1201 (attached to the turnout) turns on the track selected by the turnout points. If you are already an experienced model railroader, you will recognize the LGB turnouts as units that function like the HO and N scale turnouts sold by Atlas and many other companies. With these turnouts, both the curved route and the straight route always have power regardless of where the points are set. This non-selective system simplifies wiring somewhat as long as you don't want to turn off power to one route by setting the points to another route.

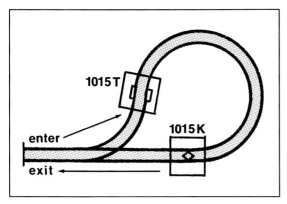

Figure 9-6: Set 1015K, for reversing loop wiring. The turnout may be spring-loaded to the entrance route.

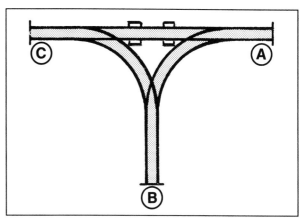

Figure 9-7: A schematic of a wye.

The power pack output into the reversing loop control switch SHOULD come from terminals unaffected by the throttle's reversing switch. When the throttle is built into the power pack, this may be impossible without breaking into the power pack case, which isn't recommended. If you must get the reversing section's power from wires controlled by the throttle's reversing switch, then set it to the same direction as the entry route while you run the train

into the insulated section, and then throw both reversing switches (the throttle's and the insulated track's) into reverse position simultaneously.

LGB has provided a means of isolating this separate segment of track, yet keeping it powered, without special wiring. A 1015T track section isolates one end of the segment and, at the other end,

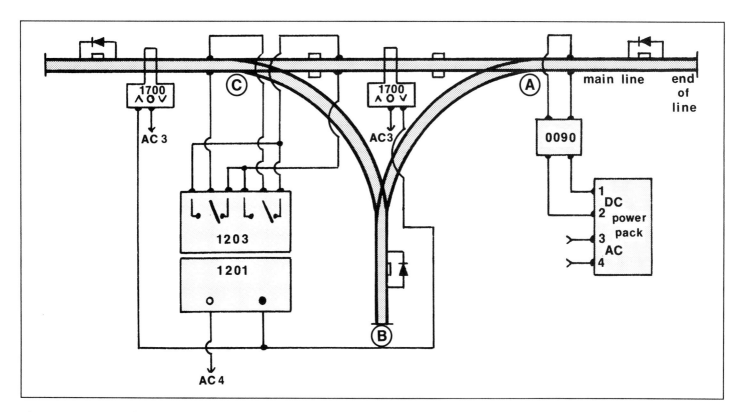

Figure 9-8: Automatic operation from a stub through a wye. All switches are spring-loaded to the left. To make a diode track, wire a diode (at least 1 amp and 50 piv for single motor locomotives; Radio Shack has one rated at 2.5 amps and 1,000 piv) across an insulating gap in one rail (5026, 1015U, or one you cut yourself with a razor saw and fill with paper glued in place and trimmed with a sharp knife). The silver band on the diode should be at the end toward which the arrow in the diagram points. Two come with the 0090 reversing unit. Note that a diode is wired into the 1203 reversing switch. The reversing unit will stop the engine for an adjustable pause, several seconds to five minutes, each of the three times it reverses in the wye and again at the other end of the line.

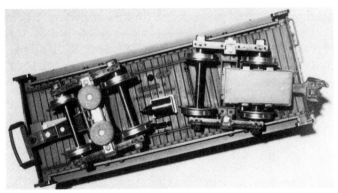

A Two Point Five Models track cleaning device (the two abrasive disks on the truck with coupler loop) and one of the 1701 LGB switching magnets (the large rectangle on the truck with knuckle coupler) are shown.

a 1015K track section feeds electricity to the segment, in one direction only.

When the 1015K is properly oriented and positioned at the exit from the isolated segment, the current in the isolated segment is set to run the train in the proper direction from entrance to exit. Thus, there is no short circuit when the engine enters from the main line into the isolated segment. When the operator or an automatic circuit reverses the main line direction, the 1015K continues to pass the same directional current to the isolated segment. When the locomotive exits, there is no short circuit on the main line, and the train is now set for travel away from the *turning section*.

Both the 1015T and the 1015K are included in the 1015K reversing loop set. (The sections are indicated in appropriate reversing loops in the track plans in Chapter 5.)

Wyes: A wye, which the Germans call a track triangle, is composed of three turnouts with their forks connected, "holding hands" as it were. To turn, a train runs through two of the switches, backs through the second and the third, and then pulls forward through the third and first. As with reversing loops, a section of track must be designated a turning track, insulated in both rails at both ends, and wired specially.

Isolate the section between turnouts C and A (see Figure 9-7). With two separate reversing switches, one for the isolated turning track and one for the rest of the wye (including the main line and turnouts A and B), an engine can be directed manually through the wye, reversing direction in the main line three times:

1. After the engine first passes turnout B, to take it back through B to turnout C;

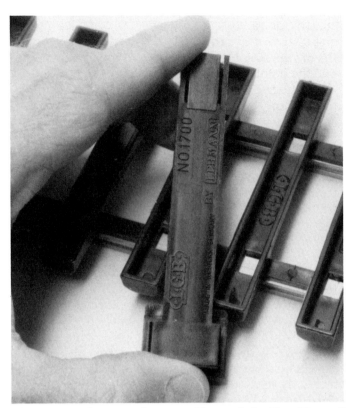

The 1700 track contact is snapped beneath the ties. The reed switch inside it is actuated by the 1701 magnet on a passing train.

2. After the engine passes turnout C, to take it back through C and the insulated section to turnout A;

3. While the engine is in the insulated turning section between turnouts C and A, so it will exit without short circuiting and continue down the main.

Obviously, the turning section must be set for travel from turnout C to turnout A. Wiring for automatic operation through a wye can be managed by using the 0090 automatic reversing unit with its two *diode* tracks, one extra diode track, and one 1201 + 1203 relay wired as a reversing switch with a diode and controlled by two 1700 track contacts (see Figure 9-8).

SIMPLE AUTOMATIC TRAIN CONTROL

Turnout-controlled track selection: For limited automatic operation through turnouts, without electricity, use the 1200 or 1210 manual turnout, which is spring-loaded to stay whichever way it is set. At a passing siding, set the turnout at one end for the main, and the turnout at the other end for the siding. Although you will have to make other arrangements for the control of the train motors (command control, block control, catenary control, or radio-battery), when the car leaves the siding area, the *turnout points* need not be thrown; the engine simply pushes through the exit turnouts, and the points will spring back to the original setting when the train has passed. If both turnouts are set to the right, trains in one direction will always take the main, trains in the other direction always the siding.

Train-operated turnout control: European model railroaders seem to enjoy fully automatic electronic controls, for hands-off operation of several trains at once through a maze of trackwork. Automatic route changes and operating signals define the routes and stop and start the trains at stations and junctions. LGB has all the devices to control such a layout, described in a number of Lehmann publications.

Briefly, the 1203 DPDT switch for routing electrical current acts as a slave to the 1201 turnout mechanism. What makes the turnout mechanism throw the turnout points and thereby change the DPDT setting? LGB offers a special track contact system that consists of a sealed 1700 *reed switch* that is placed beneath the track. A 1701 magnet is attached beneath a locomotive or car to operate the electronic reed contact automatically as the train passes. The contact can be used to operate the turnouts automatically.

If the 1201 electromechanical switches are fitted with the *slave* 1203 electrical switches, and they in turn are wired to turn power to various track sections on or off, then the 1700 reed and 1701 magnet pair can be used to start and stop trains automatically at stations or sidings. (The train's 1701 magnet turns on the 1700 track contact, which operates the 1201 turnout motor, which moves not only the turnout points but also the slave 1203 DPDT, which then feeds current to the insulated track section.) If the 1203 DPDTs are wired not to rails but to signals, the 1700 with 1701 track contacts can control the signals. In fact, signal control and track power control can be routed simultaneously through separate poles of the same 1203 switch.

Insulating one or both rails can be done to control trains automatically. If a stub siding is attached to a turnout's diverging route with a track section with one 1015U insulated rail, a train can be automatically prevented from leaving the siding when the turnout is set against it. A 1203 DPDT switch that attaches to the 1201 turnout motor changes setting as the turnout point rails are moved to shift the track routing. Simple wiring, using only two connections on the 1203, and treating it as an *SPST* (single pole, single throw) on-off switch, routes power through the 1203 switch and across the gap in 1015U only when the turnout is set correctly. That allows the turnout, for example, to hold a second train on a stub-ended siding or a siding with a track section insulated at both ends until the turnout is thrown to allow the train to proceed out of the siding (see Figs. 9-4, 9-5).

By using two more 1015U insulated tracks in the main line beyond the turnout fork, it too can be protected from running into a turnout set against it.

Lehmann's "Layouts and Technical Information" has an elegant circuit for automatic polarity control between two reversing loops, using a spring-loaded turnout in one loop, in the other loop a 1201-powered turnout with a 1203 power-routing switch, and three 1700 track contacts operated by a 1701 magnet on the locomotive (see Figure 9-9).

For manual rather than automatic remote control of turnouts you can operate up to four turnouts individually with the four switches in the 5075 Lehmann control box or construct your own. However,

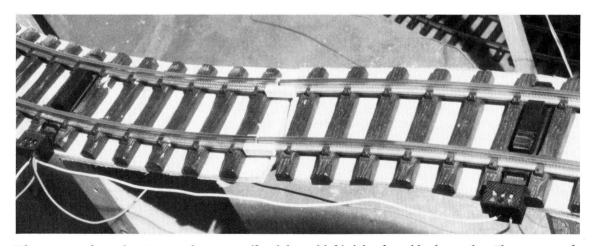

Wires are run from the 1700 track contacts (far right and left) right alongside the tracks. These two track sections are joined with two of the 5026 insulated rail joiners. They are all part of the LGB circuit to throw the turnout automatically at a reverse loop.

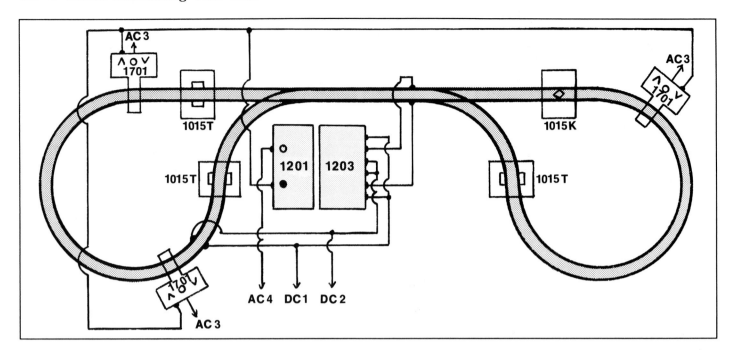

Figure 9-9: Main line current is reversed whenever the turnout at left is thrown by 1201. Turnout at right is spring-loaded. With this circuit, the train can run through the loops continuously without attention.

because of the special kind of current the 1201 EPL turnout mechanisms use (not DC, direct current, or AC, alternating current, but *half-wave direct current*), you should consult the Lehmann manual. All it takes is adding a diode or two and a switch for each turnout, so experienced hobbyists may want to make their own.

POWER DISTRIBUTION

So far, this chapter has discussed what happens in and around the rails. Although rail connections are still involved, train control usually focuses on what happens *before* the electricity reaches the track.

Independent train control (not just turning locomotives on or off, but independently regulating their speed and direction) can be accomplished several ways. (These discussions ignore the special requirements of turning tracks, such as reversing loops; they must always be provided for, as discussed on page 80 and in the section on command control, on page 88.)

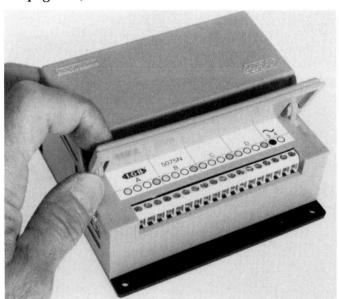

The push buttons in the 5075 control box are used to actuate remote-control turnouts. The hinged lid over the buttons and the lid over the wire-connecting terminals at the back allow the box to remain outdoors in all seasons.

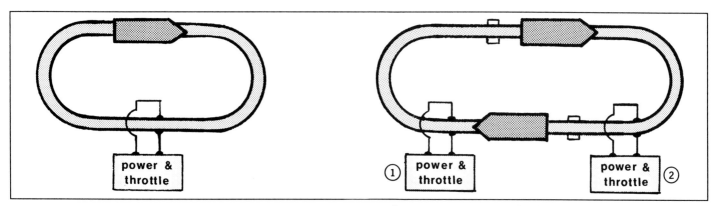

Figure 9-10: Power routing for one train.

Figure 9-11: Power routing for section control, two trains.

One train: To control just one train, only a power pack and two wires are needed. (Please note: this is true except for turning tracks!) If you have one or more locomotives on the layout at once, you should provide at least one holding or storage siding for each locomotive to be parked, plus at least one more. The extra one is for the locomotive currently running when you decide to park it and operate a different one.

Section control: Section control splits the rail system into two or more electrically separate units, and controls each with a separate power pack. Section control is the easiest to install, and the least satisfactory to operate. It works best for spectators who have several continuous routes, on which they operate trains that never ride the same rails. Typi-

cally, a single or double connecting track (see Figure 4-23) makes an infrequent swapping of routes possible, but it is awkward. This system is popular in Europe, where the spectator role is more common, and is the system for controlling large layouts represented in Lehmann books.

When crossing a train from one power pack's section to another, you can (a) set both packs at low speed, so engine surge will be less galvanic as it momentarily gets power from both packs; (b) turn the second pack off, turning it back on after the engine is fully in the new territory and has stopped running; or (c) make a short transitional block, with its own DPDT switch, that can be controlled by either pack, following the procedure for wiring block control. Do NOT run a train from one section to the next when

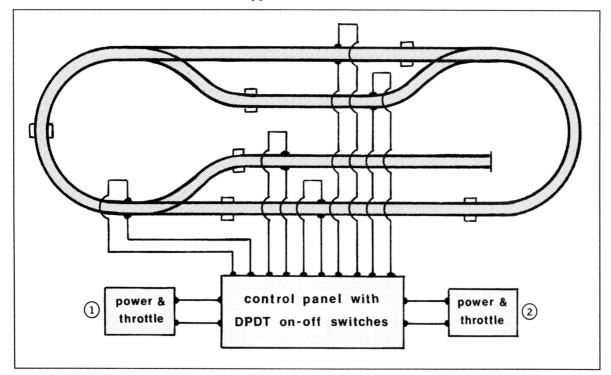

Figure 9-12 Power routing for block control, two trains. For independent control of more than two trains, replace the DPDT center-off switches with two-pole, multiple-throw rotary switches (as many throws — poles — as trains, plus off).

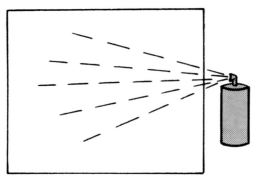

1. Spray the board a light color such as yellow.

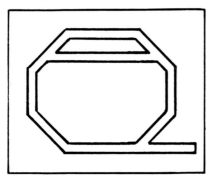

2. Attach 1/4" strips of masking tape in a schematic of the track plan. If space permits, use 1/2" for the main line, 1/4" for sidings and branch line.

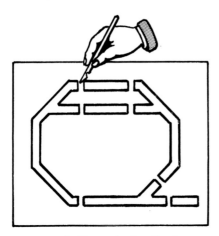

3. With a sharp knife or single-edged razor, cut 1/8" gaps dividing the plan into blocks to match the locations of those gaps in the track itself.

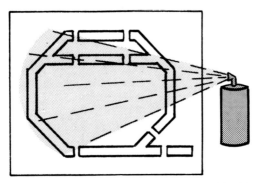

4. Spray the board a dark color, such as green-black (use a can of green and one of black, mixing on the board, if the color is not available).

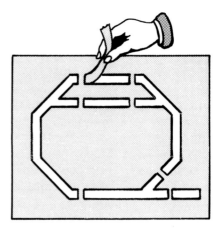

5. Peel off the tape.

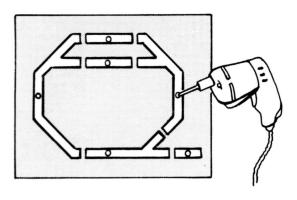

6. Drill holes to install block switches (DPDT center-off).

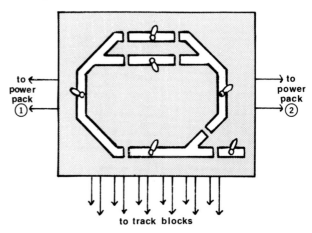

7. Add wiring and mount between power packs.

FIGURE 9-13:
MAKING A CONTROL PANEL

the two power packs are set for opposite directions! The resulting short circuit, an unpleasant hazard of this system, may damage equipment, although circuit breakers in most power packs reduce this risk.

Block control: Modelers in many scales use block control (Figure 9-12), or cab control. The track's rails are cut, electrically, into many pieces, each of which has its own switch to connect it in turn to as many power packs as there are trains running simultaneously (that is, one power pack per train). The cuts are simply insulating breaks in the 1015 track or pairs of 5026 insulating rail joiners.

With a complex layout (complexity is determined by the number and relationship of switches), block control can mean a lot of wiring. In addition, one operator must stay at the control panel (which you will have to make for yourself — see Figure 9-13) to throw the block selection switches.

A simple and very practical form of block control limits the number of trains to two, so very common and inexpensive DPDT switches can be used as block selectors (see Figure 9-14). Each individual connection is simple, so if you work one block at a time, installation is not difficult.

Use center-off DPDT switches, so that most blocks are left turned off with their selectors in the center-off position. Locomotives can then be parked at various points around the layout, with all selector switches in the center-off position except the two blocks in which trains are running and the two blocks where they are respectively headed.

A good place to insulate, creating new blocks, is in the diverging tracks of a turnout, so that after a train goes through the turnout onto, for example, the

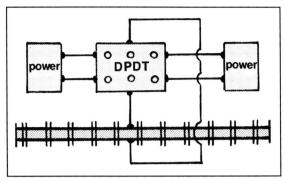

Figure 9-14: Wiring of a single block selector switch. This DPDT switch, unlike Lehmann's 1203, is center-off. Switches with toggle levers usually come with contacts arranged like a six-spot on dice, with the two center contacts to be connected to the track, and each end pair to one power pack. Throwing the toggle handle connects the center pair to one of the end pairs, usually to the end pair it points away from.

straight route, it can relinquish control of the turnout to a following or meeting train that wants to go through the turnout on the curved route. Kalmbach publishes an excellent book, **How to Wire Your Model Railroad,** which discusses the many possible ramifications of this kind of control; or see **The HO Model Railroading Handbook,** Volume I of **The Model Railroading Handbook** series published by Chilton, or books published by Atlas for their HO and N scale trains.

Note that this same system of providing on-off switches for electrically isolated blocks can be used with stub-ended sidings or passing sidings to provide places to hold additional locomotives.

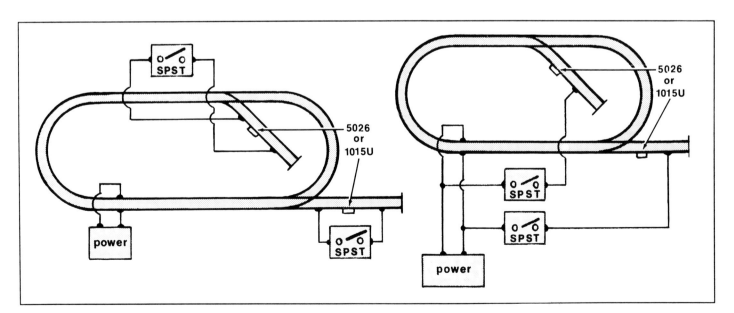

Figures 9-15 and 9-16: Loop with two stubs for parking engines. The one on the left shows wiring if the switches are at the track; the right one shows wiring if the switches are at a control panel.

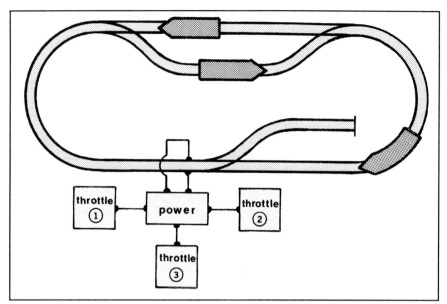

Figure 9-17: Power routing for command control, three or more trains.

Voltage differential control: Since some LGB engines will start moving at a lower voltage than others, a limited two-train control option allows running the low-voltage engine while the high-voltage engine (a feature Lehmann calls EAV) waits in the same electrical block. Thus, a road engine might pull its train into a station where a low-voltage switcher waits in a parking track (with an on-off switch). The

switcher could then do low-speed switching chores, altering the main line train's consist, without moving the high-voltage road engine. If voltage is increased too much, both engines will move in the same direction. The EAV technique is not true independent train control, but has the great advantage of requiring no special wiring beyond a parking track.

Carrier/Command-Control: For most modelers, carrier/command-control, or command control, is a black box system. A single power pack, with a single pair of connecting leads to the track, sends all locomotives power to run as well as a coded message telling them how fast and in which direction (see Figure 9-17). Engines must be fitted with decoders that intercept the track current on its way to the motor.

Command control is expensive, and installing the receivers in the engines can be a problem, especially for someone who has never disassembled an engine. Most installation instructions, coming from the command control manufacturer and not from Lehmann, are generic rather than specific to LGB. You will have to figure out for yourself where to break the engine's electrical circuits and where to locate the control receiver. (Many hobby shops will arrange installation for a fee.) Command control does give the most prototypical control, because it gives the greatest independence of operation. You can, however, run two engines into each other at full speed, which is virtually impossible in other systems. The ability to run many different locomotives on the same rails makes command control unique.

Different systems use different kinds of electronic codes, but all can send a dozen or more different

Common Rail Wiring

Some wire and one pole per block control switch can be saved for two-train block control by *common rail* wiring. One rail, the same throughout the entire track system (not turning tracks), is designated the common rail, and is permanently wired to one DC output from each power pack.

The common rail has no block insulators. The other rail in each block is wired separately through a SPDT switch, or one pole of a DPDT switch, and connected as the toggle is thrown to either pack. If DPDT switches are used, that leaves the other pole of the switch for indicator lights in a panel, if desired. See the books mentioned in the text for a fuller discussion.

LGB's **catenary system** is a form of common rail wiring, with one rail of the track serving as the common rail, and the overhead wire and the other rail acting as permanently distinct block wires permanently connected to separate power packs. Because LGB pantograph locomotives when set to catenary operation always disconnect wheels on the same side, the locomotives cannot turn around as on a reversing loop and still be controlled via the catenary.

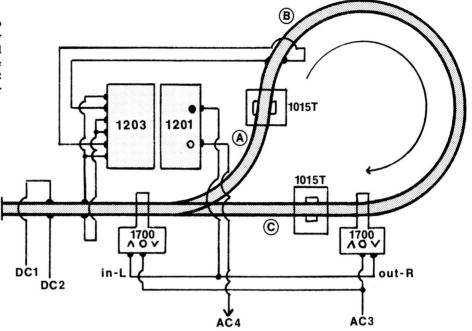

Figure 9-20: Reversing loop wiring for automatic polarity control in a command control power system, running clockwise only, as shown. Letters A, B, C identify new 1700 locations for two-way operation; see text.

Reversing Loops with Command Control.

All types of control require an insulated section (both rails at both ends) in a reversing loop. With most types of control, once the engine with all other metal wheel electrical pickup cars is in the insulated section, you need to reverse the direction of the current in the main line to continue out of the insulated section.

With command control, you can reverse the current in the insulated section, while the train is in it. The train will keep moving in the same direction, without pausing, and there will be no short circuit through the wheels as it exits the insulated section. The advantage is simply a saving in wire. When two reversing loops are at either end of your backyard, you don't have to run wire from both of them to the main line reversing switch, as you do with conventional control.

To reverse the current automatically in a command control reversing loop with LGB parts, wire DPDT 1203 as a reversing switch (see Figure 9-19), and operate it as a relay with switch drive 1201, controlled by 1700 track contacts placed just in front of the 1015T or two 5026s insulating break. If the loop will only be traversed in one direction, use two track contacts (in-L and out-R; see Figure 9-20). For travel in either direction add two more track contacts (in-R and out-L) at C and B respectively; move contact in-L to A; and disconnect 1201 from the turnout. The two L (left) contacts, wired identically, set the 1201 and 1203 relay to feed the insulated section of track the same polarity as the left-hand main line fork; the two R (right) contacts, wired alike, reverse the relay to match the insulated section to the right-hand fork of the main line.

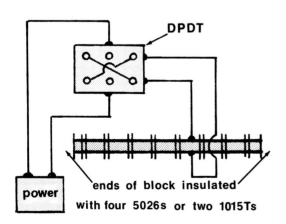

Figure 9-18: Reversing switch wiring for a DPDT toggle switch; electrically equal to Figure 9-19.

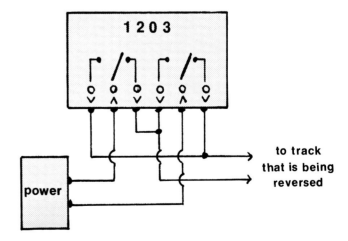

Figure 9-19: 1203 LGB DPDT wired as a reversing switch; electrically equal to Figure 9-18.

coded messages at once. That means that a dozen or more locomotives can be operated at the same time, on the same track, each one under completely independent control from every other. In most systems, booster power supplies must be added for a large number of engines.

For a throttle, the Dynatrol system uses a small box with a knob, while the Onboard system uses a small key pad similar to a hand-held calculator. These boxes are on electrical wire tethers that let you walk as much as twenty feet from the control panel, to stay closer to your train. For true walkaround control, a feature loved by engineers, a radio such as those for model airplane control can control the throttle.

Once a receiver has been installed in each locomotive on the track (following the control system instructions, LGB disassembly diagrams, and your own ingenuity), the main power pack can be connected to the track with just two wires. No additional insulating gaps or blocks are needed except, as always, for reversing loops, wyes, and turntables. Block selector toggles need not be thrown as the train progresses around the layout.

If you are operating alone, set the speed for the second locomotive and it will continue to run at that speed regardless of how you alter the speed or direction of the first locomotive. The entire operation is much more like real railroading because you must watch out for other trains and turnouts set incorrectly, or if you have them, for signals.

Note that if you allow locomotive headlights and taillights to pick up current directly from the track, a command control system may keep them fully lighted at all times. To get automatic on/off or bright/dim reversing of lights when the locomotive reverses, you will have to intercept the lights' connections when installing the receiver in the locomotive, and feed them the same current that the motor receives.

NIGHT LIGHTING AND OTHER EFFECTS

All of the LGB power packs and the Model Rectifier, Polks/Aristo, and Starr/Tri Tec power packs have separate AC circuits that can be used to power such accessories as remote-control electromechanical turnouts (1201), signals (5091-94), streetlights (5050, 5055, 5056), yard lights, wall lights, lighted street clocks, building interior lights, windmill or carousel or water mill motors, crossing gates with a crank-turning caretaker, and billboards with running lights. (Pola and Model-Power make most of these accessories.) But if you have many of these accessories, current drain on your power pack can

A control panel has been made from hardboard with a track diagram and simple toggle switches to actuate the remote-control turnouts. The Keller Onboard carrier/command-control system was built into the edge of the panel. The two key pads are the Onboard controls for two locomotives.

be substantial, and you may wish to have an independent low-voltage (12-18 v.) AC power source.

A small village with a few streetlights and the warm glow of lighting from the stores, houses, and station is a delightful sight on a model railroad, indoor or outdoor. Most bulbs operated on full voltage give a too bright and white light. Operate the bulbs at a lower voltage than their rating, and their yellower color will look more realistic.

Track current, of course, operates lights aboard the trains. The LGB locomotives are all equipped with working headlights that are bright enough to throw a realistic beam of light down the track ahead of the train. The LGB Moguls and some of the four-drivered locomotives (2010 and 2015) are fitted with sockets to allow plug-in connections for the lights in passenger cars and cabooses, which may be added with a 3030 light conversion kit (two for four-axle cars, one for two-axle cars).

Chapter 10
Couplers and Switching Operations

It is great fun to watch a model train snaking its way around the track and through the scenery. In time, though, that around-and-around operation can become monotonous when you no longer feel like being a spectator. You can add some excitement to the operations by creating a layout, like those in Chapter 3, that provides a variety of different train routes; imagine yourself a dispatcher, routing trains through signal-protected intersections to different lines and destinations.

You can get just as much enjoyment by adding a few turnouts to an existing layout, making stub ended sidings. Imagine yourself an engineer, traveling with the locomotive as it delivers and picks up cars at various destinations. Now, you can vary the makeup of the train, delivering cars with imaginary loads needed at a track side industry or freight house, or leaving empty cars to be loaded with imaginary products to be shipped elsewhere; later picking up the newly emptied or loaded cars, left during an earlier run-by, and ready now to be moved elsewhere. The real railroads and modelers call it switching, a delightful game that you can begin to enjoy by adding just one turnout and a few feet of track.

The LGB mogul on the lower track is pushing a pair of converted high-sided gondolas (see Chapter 12) toward a facing point turnout (out of sight to the right) on Norm Grant's layout.

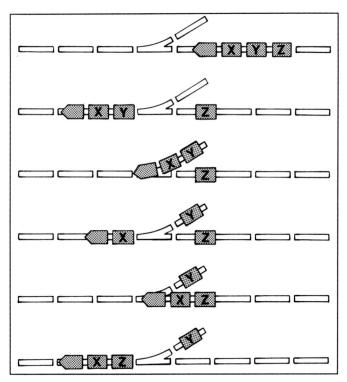

Figure 10-1: Switching a trailing point turnout. Since car Y is to be spotted in the siding, car Z must be dropped out of the way and then picked up when the train is ready to proceed.

REAL RAILROAD SWITCHING MOVES

Real railroads do not assemble trains by lifting up a car off one track, hoisting it through the air wheels a-dangle, and plopping it down behind the locomotive or another car on the next track. Only modelers assemble trains by this "big hook" method. Real railroads use two or more parallel tracks connected by a turnout so the locomotive can arrange the cars into a train or park them while it goes on its way. The simplest of these moves takes place if the car is to be switched or, as the real railroads call it, "spotted" at a *trailing point* switch.

All the crew needs to do is to throw the turnout's points from the main line direction to the siding. The locomotive then backs the boxcar into the cattle siding, stops, uncouples, moves forward, waits for the brakeman to throw the switch back to the main line setting, and then proceeds forward down the track.

Nearly all the switching moves in the giant modern freight yards are performed with variations of this simple trailing point switch movement, the engine often pushing a string of cars over a "hump," a small hill leading to a fan of remotely operated trailing point turnouts, so that cars uncoupled at the crest coast onto the right track, following a turnout path set remotely by a tower operator. (Nowadays, machines scan the reporting markings on the car side as it crests the hump, and a computer sets the turnout route automatically.) Sometimes, there may be strings of dozens of cars to be sorted for different destinations, or to be moved from one siding to another, or to be removed from an arriving train or added to a departing train.

Most real narrow gauge operations are on a smaller scale. If a few switches are all you have room and money for, you are following the example of these lines. Note that with a model railroad, uncoupling ramps — the number and location depending on the brand of coupler — must be installed in the track if the couplers are not operated manually.

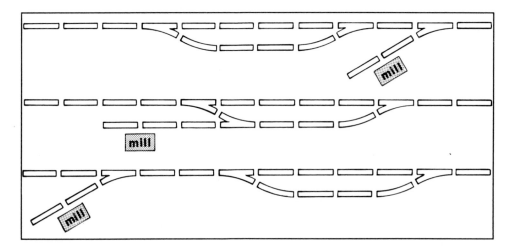

Figure 10-2: For a train traveling from right to left, engine in normal position at the front, the mill turnout in all three cases is a facing point turnout; to spot a car at the mill, the engine must run around the car and push it into the siding, as in Figure 10-3.

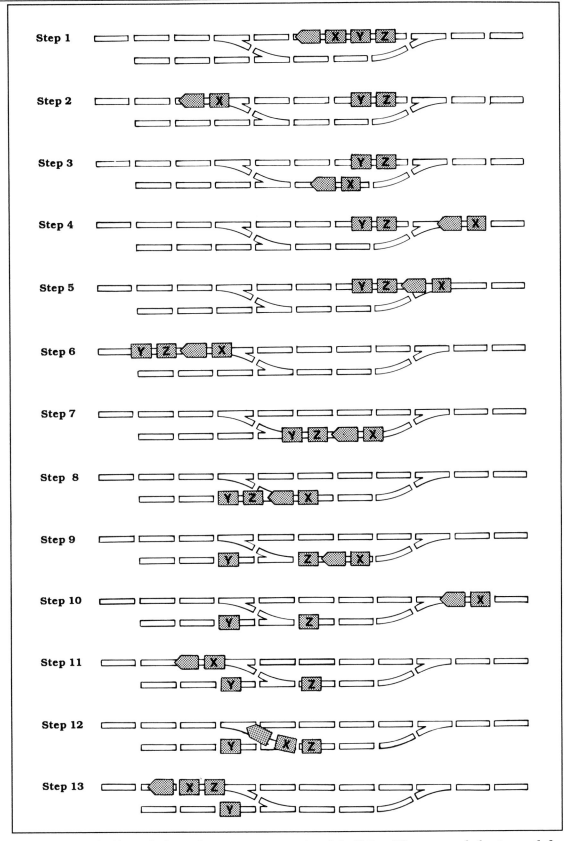

Figure 10-3: Switching a facing point turnout. Steps 1 and 2: if the siding were only long enough for one car, or if Z were many cars, Z would have to remain behind at the right, far enough away from the right-hand turnout to leave room for the engine and X in step 4. In that case, steps 9 through 13 would consist simply of backing all the way to the right to get Z and the rest of the train, and then proceeding down the main line to the left.

The Delton Locomotive Works operating knuckle coupler (right) is designed to replace the standard LGB coupler using the LGB attaching screw. LGB's 2019/2 coupler is nearly identical in appearance.

THE FACING POINT RUNAROUND

Switching a trailing point turnout is simple. If, however, the car in Figure 10-1 is to be spotted at a facing point turnout, the switching movements get far more complex. The engine must uncouple the car that is to be set out, leaving it in a double-ended siding or runaround track (see Figure 10-2). The engine then runs around the car through the turnouts at both ends of the siding, so that the car becomes the head of the train and can be pushed into the facing point siding (see Figure 10-3).

Only one of the couplers on each LGB car has the hook below the loop but additional hooks are available if you prefer non-polarized cars that can be coupled and uncoupled even if turned around.

The runaround siding may be any distance from the facing point siding where the car is to be spotted. A freight train that operates as a switching local, leaving the yard and returning the same day, may choose to drop or pick up cars only at trailing point sidings; when the train turns around to come back — the engine relocated, perhaps tender first, at what used to be the tail of the train — what were facing point sidings on the way out are trailing point sidings on the way home.

Also, when the train is assembled in the yard, the cars may be carefully ordered so that the first car to be dropped is last, the next car to be dropped is next to last, and so forth. That simplifies the procedure shown in Figure 10-3, since the trailing car, Z, is eliminated.

Note that an oval can double as a runaround track. If the tracks with the arrows at the extreme left and right (the main line) are connected to form an oval, then the runaround siding would be optional, especially in a small layout. A locomotive can simply uncouple from the car near the points of the facing turnout and travel on around the oval to the rear of the car, so it can be pushed into the siding.

COUPLER TYPES

Couplers in use on LGB trains are either hook-and-loop or knuckle couplers. LGB cars come equipped by Lehmann with hook-and-loop couplers. (Lehmann also has a replacement knuckle coupler, 2019/2.) The company engineers have refined the design of the early models to achieve a better grip, a wider coupling range on curves, and the possibility of hooks at both ends. For someone who favors continuous running and the spectator role, instant availability may be more important than their unrealistic appearance.

While Lehmann announced a knuckle coupler in its 1988-89 catalogue, they are also offered by two other manufacturers, Delton and Kadee. All look like real American couplers. The mechanical operation of the Delton coupler is more prototypical, and will appeal to an operator doing hands-on uncoupling. The LGB 2019/2 couplers also have prototypical action plus they will uncouple over any LGB 1052 and 1056 uncoupling ramp.

The Kadee knuckle couplers have an impressive and unrivaled reputation for reliable operation, in scales ranging down to the near microscopic Z scale. A prototype modeled to one foot in LGB scale would be about one and a quarter inches in Z scale. The delayed action feature and the mechanical reliability of the Kadee appeal to operators with remote uncouplers as they operate the throttle.

Any of the three coupler brands can be coupled together by lifting the cars, but none will couple or uncouple with another brand automatically.

LGB HOOK-AND-LOOP COUPLERS

Each LGB locomotive and car is fitted with automatic couplers. (Some locomotives, particularly American prototypes with cowcatchers, have no usable front coupler, typical of some road engines not used for runaround switching operations.) Only one of each car's two couplers is fitted with a coupling hook, however, which polarizes the cars: the two ends are not equivalent for coupling. Polarization means that the cars must be oriented so that all the ends with the hooks, for example, are pointed toward the end of the train. Having only one hook makes it easier to uncouple the cars, since only one hook must be disengaged.

Coupling is accomplished merely by pushing two cars or a car and locomotive together while both are on the track. Obviously, that coupling can be done by remote control, using the locomotive.

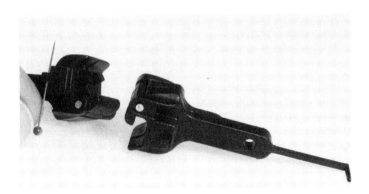

The vertical plastic pin is used to actuate the Delton coupler like the similar pins on prototype couplers. It is easier to move the small pin if you use an ice pick or a hat pin inserted into the hole in the top of the plastic pin. LGB's 2019/2 couplers can also be uncoupled automatically using the 1052 or 1056 uncoupling ramps.

Turning tracks (reversing loops, wyes, and turntables) require that coupling be de-polarized, or eventually cars you want to couple will meet hookless loop to hookless loop, with nothing to hold them together. Separate hooks now are included with most LGB cars, or they are available as accessories if you want hooks on both ends of all cars. Note that the old style of coupler, provided on cars manufactured before 1979, do not have the lateral movement required by two hook couplers going around a tight curve. Therefore, if you are double hooking all your cars, you should replace all old-style couplers. This usually means replacing the old *truck* as well, since the older couplers were integrally part of the truck. (Save old

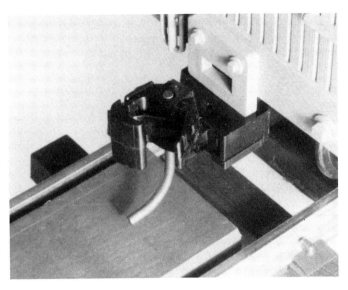

The Kadee uncoupling ramp is a simple magnet that is available either as a separate piece or, shown, installed in a section of LGB track. The coupler is still in the coupled position, here.

trucks and couplers for sale to a collector, either by themselves as parts or to be reinstalled.)

Uncoupling can be done either by hand or with an uncoupling ramp. LGB offers two types of uncoupling ramps, the 1052 snap-in permanent ramp that fits between the rails over the ties, and the 1056 remote-controlled uncoupling ramp, sold mounted in a 150 mm 1015 track section.

The couplers will not uncouple when the train passes over the permanent ramp unless the train slows almost to a halt, to give the coupler hook time to disengage before it swings back into coupled position. If both couplers have hooks, two of the permanent ramps will be needed, so that both couplers'

The magnet repels the steel uncoupling pin to swing it to the side, and that opens the coupler's face. The two couplers will not actually uncouple, however, until there is some slack or free play between the cars.

hooks disengage at once. The remote-control ramp is operated by pushing a button to raise the ramp electrically. This, in turn, lifts the hook's pivot to disengage the couplers. The 1015 remote ramp will also uncouple the cars even if both couplers have hooks.

THE DELTON KNUCKLE COUPLER

Both LGB and Delton Locomotive Works offer replicas of the knuckle-style coupler used on full-sized American cars and locomotives. Both couplers operate almost like real railroad couplers with a hinged knuckle that is locked with a vertically sliding pin. When that pin is pulled upward, the coupler opens. The couplers do, however, have a small tab inside that allows them to couple or close automatically. To open them, for manual uncoupling, the plastic pin must be pulled upward. It is easier to reach the pin if you insert a tiny ice pick into the holes in the top as shown in the photo on page 95.

KADEE'S DELAYED ACTION COUPLERS

Kadee couplers are the most popular automatic couplers with experienced HO and N scale model railroaders. The unusual design looks like a real knuckle coupler, but a long wire below the coupler is used to pivot the coupler jaw open — there is no vertical locking pin. This wire is moved by the repelling force of a permanent magnet that is placed between the rails. The magnet is the uncoupling "ramp" with Kadee's couplers. The couplers will couple anywhere by simply pushing two of them together.

The Kadee couplers will uncouple over the magnetic ramp but the locomotive must back up a fraction of an inch to leave some slack between the couplers of the parting cars. If, however, the locomotive stops over the ramp to cock the coupler open, and reverses slightly, the car can then be pushed on

forward for any distance beyond the ramp without the coupler recoupling. This is Kadee's patented "Delayed Action" which allows you to use far fewer uncoupling ramps. When the car is at its destination, the locomotive stops, then reverses, and the couplers will remain uncoupled to leave the car at the siding.

It does take a bit of care in performing smooth switching moves to make the Kadee couplers operate since the short reverse move is needed to introduce slack between the couplers so they will uncouple. Most model railroaders find that the Kadee couplers allow them to duplicate nearly all the real railroad switching moves with extremely high reliability of the couplers uncoupling just where and when they want.

LOCATING UNCOUPLING RAMPS

If you are using either hook and loop or knuckle-style LGB couplers, you will need an uncoupling ramp every place a car is to be uncoupled: at the clearance point (where a car will not foul trains passing on the main line) of each stub siding (A and B in Figure 10-4) and where cars are to be left while the engine runs around them (at least at K1 in 10-4). If the switching is to be done only by trains traveling to the left, locate the coupler near the left turnout of the runaround. If switching will be done by trains going both ways, add an uncoupler at the other end of the siding (O in 10-4). Dropping the rear of the train to switch the middle (as in Figure 10-1, where there is no runaround; and in Figure 10-3, to avoid extra moves taking car Z back to the uncoupler at K1) requires additional ramps, at C (for 10-1) and at K2 (for 10-3).

If you are using Kadee couplers, fewer ramps are needed. In Figure 10-4, only the ramps K1 and K2 are necessary; the ramps at A and B are unnecessary. The locomotive, however, needs to pull the car forward so the couplers are over ramp K1 to leave the car in the trailing point siding, beside the cattle pen

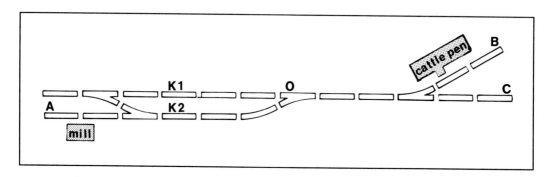

Figure 10-4: The location of uncoupling ramps that allows the locomotive to run around the boxcar so the car can be pushed into the sidings at A and B. A, B, and K1 are the minimum locations for uncoupling ramps. (See text.)

at B. For a car in the middle of the train, it can either push the tail, Z, back from ramp K1 to position C, before returning to K1 to cock the coupler open and pushing Y to the cattle pen; or it can drop Z at K1, run around Z, pausing at K2 to cock Y's coupler, and then push Y to the cattle pen.

The same moves are used for the runaround maneuver for the facing point switch to get the car into that siding, at the mill near A. Here, the ramp K2 is used to cock the couplers so the car can be spotted at the mill. The train stops while pushing a cocked coupler (as though to let the crew throw a turnout) near A, but the stop has to be gentle enough so no slack is introduced between the couplers. Otherwise, the car recouples when the locomotive starts forward again.

INSTALLING KADEE COUPLERS

Kadee offers a variety of different couplers for LGB models that allow the coupler to be mounted either on the trucks as shown in the photographs or in the more realistic position on the bottom of the car body. To mount the number 831-834 couplers, remove the screw that retains the LGB coupler; then cut off the small dimpled end of the mounting pad as shown in the Kadee instructions. The Kadee coupler can then be attached with a single screw.

The Kadee coupler pocket is attached in the standard LGB coupler mounting position.

The bottom of the simulated brake hose (the wire trip pin) must be exactly 1/8 inch above the Kadee ramp's magnet. A wood clothespin in the photograph shows where it is 1/8 inch thick. When the clothespin is pushed gently between coupler and ramp, you can tell if the wire trip pin is too low or too high by where it first contacts the tapered clothespin. The wire trip pin can be bent upward or downward with pliers to obtain the correct height.

The Kadee 831-834 coupler parts (bottom) must be assembled before the coupler is mounted on the LGB truck.

Mark the place where a wood clothespin is exactly 1/8 inch thick, to use the clothespin as a gauge to check the Kadee coupler pin height.

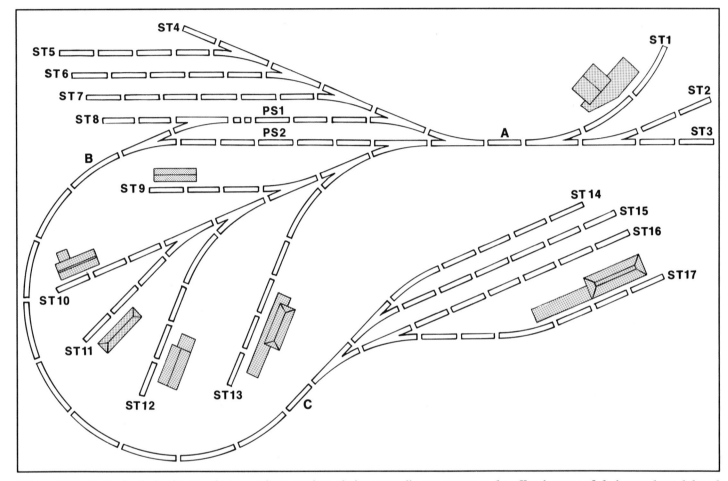

Figure 10-5: Kadee includes instructions on where to place their uncoupling ramps to make effective use of their couplers' delayed action feature, which requires pushing the car from the uncoupling ramp into the track where it will be dropped or spotted (parked). If the engine is on the right end of the car, the single ramp at A allows you to spot cars at stub tracks ST4-8, 9-13, and 14-17. The passing sidings (PS1 and PS2) will allow the engine to drop a car temporarily on PS1 and run around it via PS2 to the desired end (left) for spotting moves at stub tracks ST1-3. An engine at the left of a car can use Ramp A to spot the car at stub tracks ST1-3. But it will need an additional ramp, B, to push the car into the passing siding (PS1) and leave it there; after running around to the right end of the car via PS2, the engine can pull the car to Ramp A and then push it to any of stub tracks ST4-17. An additional ramp at C is convenient but not necessary for spotting cars at stub tracks ST14-17.

Chapter 11
Structures

R eal railroads exist to serve the customers and communities along the rail line. A model railroad exists solely for the pleasure of the operators and spectators. And yet a model railroad will seem far more credible if there is some evidence that it, too, serves customers and communities. The evidence of such a need for service is the structures visible beside any real railroad. A railroad station added to a scene, for example, dramatically increases its realism. The station implies that there are passengers and baggage and, perhaps, freight that moves inside the cars of the railroad.

BUILDINGS TO WEATHER THE STORM

If you leave any structure out in the weather all year, even if it's the house you live in, it is going to fade and chip and generally need extra maintenance. In fact, you would be wise not to leave a treasured model outside. Charles S. Small, author of numerous books about narrow gauge trains and of the first article on an American LGB layout, lost a bridge representing hundreds of hours of work, complete with working expansion bars, to a falling tree limb.

Although few items can tolerate falling trees, most of the structures and kits made for use with LGB trains are formed from plastic that can withstand extremes in temperature as well as sunlight and water. Some of the American-made kits are plywood, which should be weather-sealed with the same paints and sealers you would use on a full-sized house. Still, most modelers who operate LGB railroads outdoors do not leave the buildings out for the entire year. They bring the structures inside before winter (or, in the sunbelt, before summer).

The most popular structures for use with LGB trains are made by Pola from West Germany. Most LGB dealers carry Pola kits. They are made of a special all-weather plastic, assembled with one of the new *cyanoacrylate* super glues. They are heavy and rugged, but they will be affected by the weather. Extreme variations in temperature can cause the plastic to expand and contract enough to break one or two of the glue joints. If that happens, they can be recemented tightly with one of the thickened hobby cyanoacrylate cements like Goldberg's Super Jet or Hot Stuff's Super T. There is nothing you can do to prevent the paint on buildings from fading but you can repaint them if and when they've faded to a chalky white. Do try to locate the structures where they are shaded from the afternoon sun by full-sized trees, fences, or your house.

Al Kincaid removed the German signs and window boxes from this 902 Pola waiting room to give it more of an American appearance.

The Train Town line of plastic building kits is available through Walthers. This is the freight station.

A FIRM FOUNDATION

It is extremely important that any model building be placed on some kind of foundation to be sure that each of its walls is perfectly vertical, even after the building has been moved repeatedly to or from the outdoor layout. The simplest foundation can be made from four half bricks, one for each corner of the structure. Set the bricks in tightly tamped soil and use a small level to be sure all four are level. Some modelers sprinkle a little concrete mix over the area and wet it, both to seal the surface and to act as a weed preventive.

ROADS

A few roads in the immediate vicinity of the buildings suggest the presence of vehicular traffic. There are numerous 1:24 scale cars and trucks available among the plastic kits if you want to add one or two to a scene — for example, waiting at a crossing. (Cars do wait at railroad crossings, but never in mid-highway — unless there has been an accident, when there is a good reason for barriers and parked police cars, both with flashing lights.)

INTERIOR LIGHTING

If you are going to run wires to the tracks and turnouts, you can certainly add a few more to the cable to provide lighting for several buildings. One of the better sources for lighting is the taillight bulbs and sockets for automobiles. The bulbs are available, for some commercial and military vehicles, in

24 volts. The 18 volts supplied by the various LGB power packs produce a warm glow in a 24-volt bulb. The LGB 5030 lighting units for passenger cars and caboose interiors can also be used inside buildings if you have trouble locating 24-volt automobile taillight bulbs.

Don't even consider using 115-volt household current to illuminate your model structures; it generates too much heat and it generally is far more difficult and dangerous to install than simple 18-volt lighting sockets. There is also danger of water causing short circuits.

CONSTRUCTING YOUR OWN BUILDINGS

The Pola and Walthers plastic buildings are all available as kits. You can use either epoxy or the thickened hobby cyanoacrylate cements to assemble the kits. Resin glue can be substituted but the model must be clamped together overnight while the cement sets.

New England Hobby Supply offers a few inexpensive wooden kits for small structures. Your LGB dealer may have some other brands that are only available in some sections of the country.

You will also find a wide range of 1:24 scale doors, windows, and house kits at many miniatures dealers. Most dollhouses are built to 1:12 scale, one inch to the foot; but there is a range of what are called half-scale or 1/2 inch dollhouses, built to 1:24 scale. There are windows, doors, and a variety of accessories in this scale. Retailers listed in the telephone book's Yellow Pages under the heading "Dollhouses

The Town Line buildings are all wood kits for a variety of small structures and accessories. This is the Crossing Shanty. They are available to dealers from New England Hobby Supply.

Industrial Miniatures makes a series of three stores, a station, and a Victorian house, all assembled and painted.

& Accessories" or "Miniatures for Collectors" stock or can order the 1/2 inch dollhouse items. There are also some milled basswood wall textures and brick surfaces in the common dollhouse 1:12 scale that are suitable for 1:24 scale structures.

When you paint a wooden structure to be used outdoors, imagine that you are going to submerge it in an ocean for a year. Yes, the same paints used for boats are suitable. And be sure to seal every surface, both inside and out. If shiny surfaces bother you, sand them lightly with very fine sandpaper to remove the sheen.

John Crompton, a professional modelmaker at Walt Disney World in Florida, has conducted workshops on simple and easy structure-building techniques. He cuts wall flats out of fiberboard, and glues them together with scraps of wood in the corner joints; any piece of scrap one-by-two or two-by-two will maintain a right-angle wall joint, as well as add strength.

He then details the buildings, following two basic principles:

1. Don't add more detail than can be seen.

2. Apply details flat.

John notes that when a building is on the ground, the viewer does not usually get closer than within a foot of it. Therefore, instead of glazing windows with glass or clear plastic, he paints the window panes a high-gloss black. The result is very convincing.

By applying details flat, John avoids the complicated construction of window openings and door-ways. He simply applies stripwood to the outer

Brad Eggemana built this grain elevator from hardboard (like Masonite) with 1/2 inch basswood interior bracing and 1/8 inch square basswood trim. The roof is sandpaper.

surface (after painting it with latex house paint) to define such things as frames, mullions, and the battens of board-and-batten construction.

SCALE PEOPLE

Realistically scaled people standing around the station platform or around any other structures lend an even greater feeling of purpose to the railroad. LGB offers a dozen sets of four to six figures each, in 1:22.5 scale; other realistic ones are made by Preiser and by Magnuson Models (available from Walthers). Noch figures, an extensive line, come clothed in cloth. 1:24 scale figures are also available for military models at hobby shops that carry plastic kits.

You can also find figures in dime stores or specialty shops if you remember that a G scale figure, three inches tall, represents a full-sized human, five feet seven and a half inches tall. Modelers have found use for inexpensive figures intended to grace wedding or birthday cakes. Some modelers feel that the most realistic figures are in stationary poses. After all, they will never move; a frozen running figure, forever immobile in midstride, dissatisfies these modelers. Like the Greek sculptor who modeled the discus thrower at the instant of pausing between backswing and forward hurl, they prefer a static position. Others like the variety of the human figure in different action poses.

Another American-made train Town Line building from Walthers: a Victorian-style Depot.

There are a number of other details, like boxes, barrels, telephone booths, hand tools, signs, and telephone poles, that can make a scene seem alive. LGB offers some of these items, and model railroad shops carry some others. Again, the plastic model kits for 1:24 scale military models often have hand tools and other detail items useful on a model railroad scene.

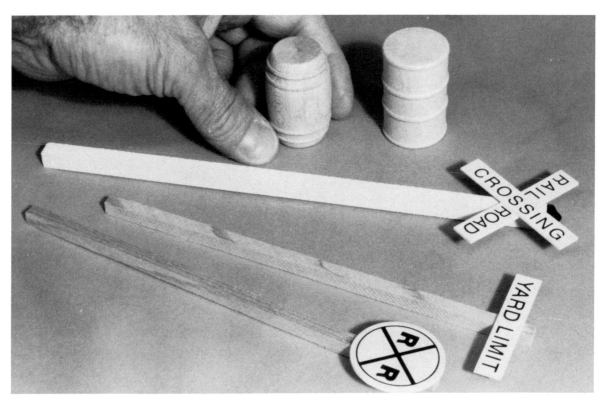

L & P Trackworks makes a variety of 1:24 scale railroad signs and barrels.

Chapter 12
Rolling Stock

Produced in Germany, LGB trains represent mostly European prototypes. Many operators in America use this equipment, some running it as is, others modifying it to resemble American prototypes.

The LGB stock car has the proper proportions and details to match the real Rio Grande cars.

LGB now produces examples of many of the common freight cars that once operated on America's narrow gauge railroads. The models include the metal wires that, on the real equipment, were threaded steel rods about 3/4 inch in diameter. The rods ran the length of the car's wooden frames with threaded ends held in place with huge square nuts. These truss rods were tightened, by turning the nuts on the ends or, more commonly, by a turnbuckle in the middle, to keep the wooden frames from sagging as the cars aged. (Sometimes they were over-tightened, and the cars would hump up a little in the middle.) Truss rods are one way that a railroad enthusiast can tell a wooden car from a metal one. Since LGB models are reproductions of real American rolling stock, some photographs of similar full-sized cars are instructive if you want to add new decals, paint, or other details.

The Rio Grande used their stock cars to move both cattle and sheep into the high mountain pastures for summer grazing.

Norm Grant converted the LGB caboose into a replica of the Colorado & Southern car using Northeastern's milled wood siding.

THE STOCK CAR

The 4068 stock car, one of the first models produced by LGB, is a very accurate replica of its American prototype model. It captures the proportions and even the positions and angles of the side and door bracing of some of the most common Rio Grande stock cars. It has molded-on grab-irons where the later *reefer* and high- and low-sided gondolas have separate grab-irons.

THE CABOOSE

The 4065 LGB caboose is probably the least accurate model in the series. It does resemble the Rio Grande's short cabooses, but these cars had trucks under each end rather than just the four wheels used on the LGB model. The Rio Grande did have some four-wheel cabooses, but they had much smaller windows and different proportions from the LGB model.

Incidentally, be careful of tunnel clearance when running this car: it was the tallest item of LGB rolling stock until the 4075 passenger/baggage/caboose combine was introduced with its cupola. But it will clear any lintel that passes the stacks of the old-prototype 2018D and 2028D Moguls.

Norm Grant used the LGB caboose as the basis for his conversion to recreate a Colorado & Southern caboose. He cut right through the roof to remove a section between the end of the cupola and the end of the body's wall. That section was added between the

The Rio Grande's short cabooses resemble the LGB model but they have eight wheels with the trucks almost hidden by the steps. Both cars are restored to authentic colors at the Colorado Railroad Museum in Golden. Notice that they differ in many details: slanted or vertical cupola side walls, presence or absence of window mullions and *fascia board*, window size, etc. MDC has a model of a similar car that operates with LGB equipment.

The LGB "Rio Grande" caboose.

cupola and the remaining roof after he had cut through the roof on the other side of the cupola. He made new walls from Northeastern's milled basswood and built a new frame for each side window.

THE REEFER

LGB offers the reefer in a variety of bright paint schemes that are based on standard gauge "billboard" refrigerator cars that operated on standard gauge railroads in the 1920s and 1930s. None of these paint schemes ever appeared on narrow gauge cars. The car is also shorter than most Rio Grande reefers. The model can be repainted, however, by removing the individual door hinges and latches so the sides can be sprayed with Floquil's Reefer Yellow, then lettered with either CDS dry transfers or Robert Dustin's decals.

THE HOPPER

In 1988 Lehmann expanded its offering of American prototype cars. The hopper introduces an eastern narrow gauge prototype, the East Broad Top (EBT). The car is appropriate for a line that did a lot of coal hauling.

LGB offers the reefer in a variety of paint schemes based on standard gauge prototype cars of the 1920s. The grab-irons and brake details are separate moldings to be installed by the modeler.

THE TANK CAR

Most of the Lehmann tank cars have been modeled on a single two-axle, European prototype, available in various colorful liveries and slightly modified through the years to bring them closer to scale, to add details, or improve construction. Their first American prototype tanker, with four axles in arch bar trucks, represents a Conoco old-timer mounted on a wooden flatcar. Other liveries are becoming available.

Most of the Rio Grande reefers were longer than the LGB model. This one is being restored at the Colorado Railroad Museum.

The Rio Grande's boxcars had the proportions of the LGB model and its end doors.

THE BOXCAR

The 4067 boxcar has many of the details, like the small square doors on the sides, of early Southern Pacific narrow gauge cars. LGB offered that paint scheme when the car was first introduced around 1978. The Rio Grande lettering scheme is that of the late 1800s. A more modern scheme would better match the other Rio Grande rolling stock, or the car could be relettered for the Denver South Park and Pacific, to match the 2028D Mogul locomotive.

THE GONDOLAS

LGB offers two Rio Grande gondolas, a 4061 low-sided car and a 4073 high-sided car. The real Rio Grande did operate both styles of cars although the low-sided cars were not photographed as often.

According to Robert Sloan's articles in the August 1981 through February 1982 issues of the *Narrow Gauge and Short Line Gazette* only about 30 of the original fleet of over 2000 low-sided cars were still in operation in the 1930s.

The LGB high-sided gondola is a reasonably accurate replica of the Rio Grande class 15 cars in number series 1500 to 1899, right down to the number on the model.

THE FLATCAR

LGB's truss rod flatcar (a discontinued 4060 which is similar to a 4169, but with a load) certainly can be considered an accurate model, if only because these cars varied so much in the design, location, and number of their stake pockets.

The draped machinery and scrap casting would make an interesting load for a model flatcar. The number of stake pockets differed on some flatcar series.

This is an earlier series Rio Grande high-sided gondola than the prototype for the LGB model; this one has slightly lower sides and fewer braces.

This LGB model is an accurate replica of the 1500-series Rio Grande high-sided gondolas.

One of the Rio Grande coaches at the Colorado Railroad Museum. The real cars were painted Pullman green during their active life on the Rio Grande.

Norm Grant used Northeastern's milled wood siding to rebuild a coach into a private or business car with an enclosed end vestibule. Both cars are painted Pullman green.

THE PASSENGER CARS

The LGB Passenger Coach and the Combined Passenger Coach and Luggage Van (discontinued as yellow "D&RGW" 3080 and 3081; now red "DSP&P" 3180 and 3181), and the newest coach/baggage/caboose (4075) are all generic designs with a shorter length and lower roof contour than any of the American narrow gauge prototypes, although the cupola makes the 4075 the tallest piece of LGB rolling stock. (Its shortness may be partly a consequence of Lehmann's commitment to producing only equipment that will run on its tightest radius curves.) The coach is similar to both Rio Grande and Colorado & Southern prototypes and the combine is a bit like the Colorado & Southern prototype. The Rio Grande did operate a combined coach/baggage/caboose on their Pagosa, Colorado line that resembled the LGB car.

The LGB combination car resembles the Colorado & Southern combines. The end platform was removed from these cars early in the century. The C & S also had coaches that resembled the LGB model.

LGB-COMPATIBLE AMERICAN CARS

Several companies offer a limited variety of LGB compatible equipment and the number is growing. Kalamazoo, Lionel, and REA offer extensive lines, including freight and passenger cars and engines. Charles Ro offers American-style freight cars in various liveries and a work train. Delton Locomotive Works has 2-8-0 locomotives, boxcars, reefers, passenger cars, some expensive brass engines, and a few wooden cars. Some companies offer just a few items, such as MDC's cabooses, ore cars, and hopper cars or Precision Scale Company's brass tank cars. (See Appendix: Supply Sources.)

EUROPEAN CARS

The Lehmann line very naturally is dominated by European prototypes. In many European countries, narrow gauge lines continue to function as revenue passenger and freight haulers, their business often bolstered by tourist travel but not dependent on it. Its diminutive size, typically much smaller than American equipment, makes it even more appealing. Most American narrow gauge common carriers used equipment at least thirty feet long, which is about 50 percent bigger than the usual European stock, amply represented by foot-long LGB cars, both passenger and freight (eg. 3010, 4035). Less typical are the long passenger cars of the modern Rhaetian Railroad (RhB) in Switzerland, which run to sixty feet and are represented by a two-foot model in LGB. Less typical too are the small ten-foot cars rarely found on com-

An LGB Boxcar before...

...and after. The LGB car has been updated to match the lettering of the stock car, gondola, flatcar, and caboose; dry transfer lettering or decals may be used.

mon carriers. The latter, only six inches in size in LGB, are usable virtually as is by someone modeling a Hawaiian plantation railroad, for example, or a private industrial facility.

Schaefer LGB Grossbahn-Center stocks a large number of post-factory modifications of LGB cars, including three- and four-axle extended 3050 compartment coaches, with and without brakemen's hut; "baby-head" cement cars, common on the RhB; long tank cars; and passenger cars repainted for various lines, with additional roof and platform details. Schaefer offers a catalogue folder with color photos (see Appendix: Supply Sources).

RELETTERING LGB MODELS

You can change the appearance of any of the LGB cars by simply changing the lettering. You may want to update the lettering on the boxcar, or you might want to letter and number the caboose or locomotive. The factory-painted lettering on the LGB models is very well applied. Be aware that your dry transfer or decal lettering will certainly not withstand the weather as well as the factory lettering, even when protected with a clear coat overlay. If you operate your relettered cars in all kinds of weather, you may

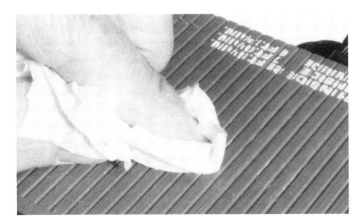

Wet a paper towel or cloth with lacquer thinner and rub the lettering just firmly enough so the lettering, and not the car side, dissolves.

eventually need to strip off the clear coat and the lettering and apply fresh lettering.

It is also possible to repaint the cars right over the factory lettering. Some modelers have used Floquil paints applied with an artist's air brush. They adhere well to the LGB plastic; a few colors are available in aerosol cans. You might also find an automotive primer color in brown or black that is suitable, but test it on a small portion of the INSIDE of the car to be certain it does not attack the plastic.

Working outdoors, you can use lacquer thinner, so the fumes dissipate, to remove the lettering from this LGB boxcar. The lacquer thinner DOES MELT THE PLASTIC, so you should use just enough to rub off the decal without destroying the detail on the car. Dip a clean rag in the fluid and rub off about 1/2 inch of the lettering at a time. Don't let the thinner drip or stand on the car side.

To apply only new road names and reporting marks (such as "D&RGW"), it is not necessary to repaint the entire car. The dry transfer sheets include accurate dimensional data as well as various car numbers, so it is almost as easy to reletter the car. In that case, the car can be repainted before lettering, covering the old markings, and you avoid damaging the car side with lacquer thinner.

DECALS OR DRY TRANSFERS?

There are two types of lettering and numbers available for these models: dry transfers or "rubons," and decals that must be soaked in water to free them from their paper backing.

CDS Lettering Limited offers a variety of dry transfers in 1:24 scale; one sheet is needed for each car or locomotive. They offer freight car, passenger car, and locomotive transfers for several narrow gauge railroads.

Tape the individual names and numbers in the proper position before rubbing over them with a blunted lead pencil.

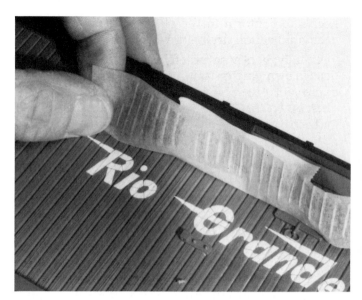

Holding one corner immobile, carefully lift the plastic backing so you can see if all the lettering has transferred. If not, hinge the plastic back in place and burnish it again.

Robert Dustin has decals for 1:24 scale (which at only 6.25 percent undersize is close to LGB's 1:22.5 scale). There are individual locomotive numbers and alphabets as well as sheets to decal specific types of freight cars. Custom decals are also available in white, black, yellow, or gold, so you can letter locomotives or passenger cars. The only heralds are for the Rio Grande and Rio Grande Southern.

Back Woods Car Shop also sells some dry transfer numbers, road names, and heralds for most American narrow gauge railroads.

Some modelers use the O scale decals sold through hobby dealers by Champ and Walthers. The 1:48 scale decals are half the size needed, but there are large lettering areas that will work for smaller lettering in 1:22.5 scale.

APPLYING DRY TRANSFERS

Dry transfers sound as if they would be easy to apply. In truth, there are some tricks to make the transfer a success.

First, cut each name, herald, or set of data from the main sheet with scissors. Cut to within 1/32 inch of the lettering. Tape the top edge of the lettering in place with a strip of masking tape so you can lift the backing without disturbing the original position of the transfer. Using a dull lead pencil or one of the special burnishing tools sold by art and drafting supply stores, gently rub every portion of the lettering; then slowly lift the backing to see if the transfer is all on the model. If some corners or chips remain on the backing, hinge it down and repeat the process. When the transfer is in place and there is no longer any lettering on the backing, remove the backing mod put a piece of paper (the one that protected the transfer is fine) on the car side so you

can rub over the paper to burnish the transfer tightly onto the side. Use a sharper pencil to tuck any edges into creases or around doors. Push over the tops of any rivets or raised details with an eraser to get the transfer snuggled tightly in place. Finally, spray on a protective coat of artist's spray fixative available from most art supply stores. Test the spray on a leftover transfer, applied to a scrap of plastic, to be sure that it does not wrinkle or melt the dry transfer.

APPLYING DECALS

There are also some tricks to be used when applying decals. Cut each decal from the sheet so you have individual heralds, road names, car numbers, and blocks of dimensional data. Dip each decal in warm water; then set it on a paper towel while the water soaks through the paper backing to dissolve the glue. When you can slide the decal on the backing, position both backing and decal on the car and hold the decal in place with the tip of a hobby knife while you slide the backing from beneath the decal with tweezers.

Decals will NOT conform to the areas between boards and around rivets unless you soften them with a decal-softening fluid such as Walthers Solvaset, Champ's Decal Set, or Micro Scale's Micro Sol, all available from hobby dealers. Brush some of the fluid on the car where you will apply the decal just before sliding the decal off its paper backing. Apply more of the fluid after the decal is in place and let the decal set for at least six hours to see if it has snuggled around the details. It may take as many as a dozen applications of the decal softening fluid to get some decals to conform to the shapes of the surface; let each application dry before applying the next.

Finally, gently scrub off any residue left from the decal's own glue or from the softening fluid, using a damp facial tissue. Let it dry overnight. The decal must then be protected with a coat of Testor's Dullcote or other clear fixative from an aerosol can.

WEATHERING MODELS

One reason that Robert Treat's and Herb Chaudiere's LGB models are so realistic is that each of them has weathered his models in addition to repainting and relettering them. The weathering is simply a very thin wash of about nine parts thinner to one part paint. Applied, it gives subtle variations in color that duplicate the effects of rain and wind-borne dirt, dust, ballast, and smoke.

You can do a reasonable job of weathering using artist's chalk-base pastels like Eberhard Faber's Nupastel or American Crayon's Prang Pastels; the usual oil-base pastels won't work. Regular chalk can be used but it may be too milky. Rub the pastels over sandpaper or scrape them with a knife to make a powder.

The pastel powder can now be applied to the car with a number 1 or 2 size paint brush. Study real railroad freight cars to see the patterns and colors you will need. Light beige or light gray dusted over the car makes it appear faded. Slight irregularity will seem more realistic than perfect uniformity. Leave a few of the scribed boards unstreaked to simulate individual boards that have been replaced, often in groups of adjacent boards. "Smoke stains" can be made by applying the powder to the underside of any raised details, like grab-irons or hinges or horizontal boards or seams, and over the entire roof. Imitate ballast and dirt kicked up by the wheels by applying black or dark brown along the lower edges of the car and about a third of the way up the ends. Create "rust" with reddish-brown (burnt sienna) or a boxcar red color, applying small splotches around the truck springs and bearing caps, to the couplers (but not the moving parts), and near the grab-irons and brake wheel.

If you want a subtle shade, use just a bit of the powder and rub it lightly. For a darker tint, use more powder and rub it in with a cotton swab like a Q-Tip. For even darker tints, wet the brush slightly with water for streaks, or use a damp cotton swab for splotches and spray patterns.

The pastels will rub off if unprotected, but you can set them by spraying lacquer thinner over the car in a fine mist using an artist's air brush. This finish must also be protected with a coat of Testor's Dullcote from an aerosol can. You can use the Dullcote directly on the pastel, to skip the use of lacquer thinner, but the pastel will fade several shades so you may want to repeat some of the weathering to obtain a darker shade. With practice, you can guess how much darker to make the weathering color, knowing how much the application of Dullcote will make it fade.

You can also weather cars and locomotives using an air brush with washes of Floquil paint and thinner, in the color shades suggested above for use with powdered pastel chalks. With an air brush, you need an air supply with adjustable pressure set to about fifteen pounds per square inch so the finest mist can be applied. Hold the air brush about six to ten inches from the model for spray or fading effects, and as close as an inch (moving the model quickly beneath the spray pattern) for streaks. Painted weathering can be applied before the use of pastel chalks, which impart the dusty effect.

Norm Grant converted a pair of LGB low-sided gondolas into a flatcar and this high-sided gondola and repainted them, then applied new decals.

Photo 12-1: To make the high-sided gondola conversion, slowly pry the red upper piece from the 4061 low-sided gondola.

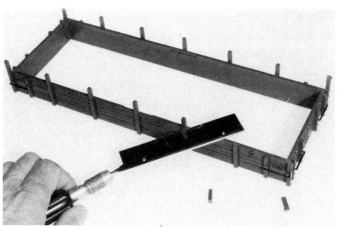

Photo 12-2: Use a razor saw to cut the protruding bottoms of each post flush with the bottom of the sides and ends.

Photo 12-3: Make a sanding block to sand the top of the second low-sided gondola (shown) and the bottom of the modified upper piece (not shown).

Photo 12-4: The upper piece (bottom) from the second low-sided gondola is ready to be installed on the second car.

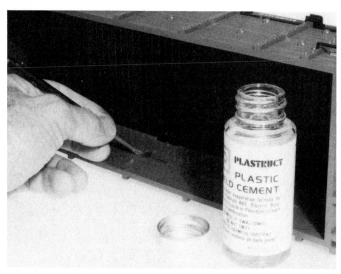

Photo 12-5: Use Plastruct's liquid plastic cement, Super T, or Super Jet, applied with an old paint brush, to join the parts.

Photo 12-6: The completed high-sided gondola conversion leaves a flatcar. You might want to change the number of one of the two cars using dry transfers.

SIMPLE FREIGHT CAR KIT CONVERSIONS

Many model railroaders modify their LGB equipment to create different types or styles of cars. Modelers running European prototype equipment will find many photos of modified LGB equipment in the issues of *LGB-Depesche*. An adventurous "chassis-basher" might try producing a three-axle car, an engineering anomaly so popular in older continental equipment and found on a wide variety of European roads, ranging from long main line French passenger cars to a tiny boxcar of the Austrian narrow gauge Zillertalbahn.

Norm Grant has a variety of modified American gondolas, cabooses, and even a passenger coach converted to a business car on his outdoor layout. Two of the 4061 LGB low-sided gondolas can be converted into a high-sided gondola and a flatcar, to create two models you cannot buy.

Gently pry the red gondola board section from the top of one of the low-sided gondolas, working around the car with a screwdriver to move it just 1/16 inch at a time (see Photo 12-1). Next, cut the stakes flush

with the bottom of the piece, using a Zona or X-Acto razor saw (see Photo 12-2). Hold the saw at an angle so the outer face of every post is about 1/64 inch longer than the inner face. It should match the angles of the tops of the posts on the second gondola. Wrap some fine grit sandpaper around a block of wood and sand the cut-off posts and the bottom of the red piece at that same angle to remove the paint. Sand the top of the second car lightly to remove the paint (see Photo 12-3). Finally, the cut gondola top can be cemented to the top of the second car (see Photos 12-4, 12-5). You need to use one of the special liquid cements intended for ABS plastic, like Plastruct cement, that are sold by hobby shops that carry plastic airplane and military models. Testor's liquid cement for plastics will not be strong enough. If you cannot locate the cement, use one of the thickened cyanoacrylate cements for hobbyists, like Goldberg's Super Jet or Hot Stuff's Super T. You can now operate the new gondola and flatcar as-is (see Photo 12-6) or repaint and reletter them. The high-sided gondola is similar to some of the cars used on the Colorado & Southern and makes an interesting variation to LGB's 4063 high-sided gondola.

Chapter 13
Locomotives

Lehmann offers a charming variety of steam, electric, and diesel locomotives based on European prototypes. Many model railroaders use these engines as prototypical motive power for European-style layouts, while others use them to suit their imaginative fancies to create unique and personal railroads.

The first "American" locomotive available from Lehmann was based on a prototype engine manufactured in Germany and exported to this country, and was marketed as 2017 with a tender added. Like most of the LGB engines, its solid *well tank* beneath a high boiler is not very American in appearance. Most American locomotives had *tenders*, and those that didn't — many of them on narrow gauge logging lines — carried their water in *side tanks* or *saddle tanks*, beside or above the boiler rather than under it. That is why Charles S. Small, in the early 1970s, used the superstructure of an LGB side-tank 0-6-2T when fashioning an 0-4-4-0T from two of the well-tank locomotives' 0-4-0 mechanisms.

LGB has produced three versions of an American Mogul with a 2-6-0 wheel arrangement consisting of a one-axle leading truck, three coupled powered axles, and no trailing truck. The first version was a model of the nineteenth century prototype with its bulging spark-arrestor stack, conical domes, wooden cab, and long pointed cowcatcher. Lettered "DSP&P", it was introduced in bright red and green (2018D). The second was its 1988-89 model, the 2028D (in Lehmann numbering, "D" stands for "dampf" or "steam," and indicates a smoking chimney), in black, brown, and gray, with a blue/gray boiler and brass- and copper-colored fittings, a red light, and cowcatcher. The third was the model of the twentieth century prototype, with its straight stack, rounded domes, generator, and short cowcatcher and was numbered 2019S. (The "S" indicates sound, in this case, bell, whistle, *chuff*, and smoking stack). All of the other LGB locomotives are based on European prototypes, although some have been offered painted for American railroads.

In addition to using the American prototype locomotives made by LGB, some modelers modify European prototypes to resemble American locomotives. The LGB 2010D locomotive resembles some

The prototype for the LGB Mogul is the number 71, built by Cooke in 1884. The factory had not yet fitted the headlight. Photo from the H. K. Vollrath Collection.

American locomotives that were used in quarry, mining, and other industrial work on narrow gauge railroads. With some black paint and a few details from firms like Short Line Foundry and Trackside Details, the model can look quite at home on American layouts. Both Herb Chaudiere and Robert Treat have used similar models to create wonderful little locomotives (see Color Plates 8 and 13).

Some modelers have created their own engine super-structures, following various prototypes, and mounted them atop one of the LGB power units. These used to be available separately, reducing expense for unused parts; though not currently listed in the LGB catalogue, some may still be available from dealers as replacement parts.

The 2035 and 2036 trolley cars resemble the two-axle *Birneys* used in some American towns, although they were not usually in narrow gauge. Narrow gauge streetcar lines are common in European cities. Lehmann offers two systems of overhead wire, one with catenary.

The little 2001 handcar, with its valiantly pumping operator, has a more solid and boxier base than most such vehicles, which tend to be spidery and more like a bicycle frame. But since they varied a good deal and might be whipped up by a railroad company's backshop, almost any version, including this one, could be justified on an American or other railroad.

THE LEGENDARY LGB MOGUL

LGB selected one of the most famous American narrow gauge locomotives as the prototype for their nineteenth century Mogul. The photo on the opposite page, taken at the Cooke Locomotive Works in Patterson, New Jersey, in February of 1884, shows the locomotive as it looked when it was built. The Denver South Park and Pacific bought it and numbered it 71. It was renumbered in 1884 to 114 and relettered to "Denver, Leadville & Gunnison". Within a year, it became Colorado & Southern number 8 and remained a number 8 until September 1939 (according to the book, *The Colorado Road*, by Hal Wagner, now out of print).

The real locomotive probably never looked like LGB's number 2018D, but it could have had the same colors as the 2028D in 1884. In about 1900, the prototype was fitted with a new boiler that tapered upward near the cab, new domes and stack, and a steel cab, so it looked much like the LGB 2019S. It may have been fitted with the same color boiler jacket as 2028D, but the other colors were probably black. Around 1906, the Colorado and

A number of American narrow gauge railroads used small mogul locomotives. This is the Nevada County Narrow Gauge Railroad's number 5 built by Baldwin in 1875. It has a snowplow replacing the pilot, a rare necessity in the California foothills. Photo taken circa 1934 at Grass Valley, California, from the Charles E. Winter Collection.

Southern adopted the silver lettering used on the LGB 2019S model.

MAINTAINING LGB STEAM LOCOMOTIVES

The only regular maintenance that an LGB locomotive needs is cleaning the drivers and pickup shoes after every eight hours of operation. Use a hard rubber eraser like a Bright Boy sold by hobby shops or a typewriter ink eraser so you do not scratch the drivers or the pickup shoe. Do not use any type of knife, file, or sandpaper to clean the drivers or the pickup, because they leave scratches that collect dirt. Wipe the drivers clean with electrical contact cleaner from an electronics hobby shop like Radio Shack or Allied.

The contact cleaner or alcohol can be used, with a pipe cleaner, to scrub around behind the drivers and around the moving connecting rods on the side of the engine. Work outdoors and away from any heat or flame. The mechanism can be disassembled to remove any accumulated dirt or grease. Follow the instructions that come with the locomotive; be careful not to lose the steel balls that serve as thrust bearings at each end of the motor armature shaft.

Hobby shops can order the LaBelle brand number 102 oil and number 106 grease, both of which are compatible with plastics. Some other oils and greases can actually soften and melt the plastic. Use just a trace of the grease on the gears, applying a dot and rotating the motor shaft to spread the grease over the gears. A single drop of the oil is enough for each bearing and crankpin (the pivot pins for the rods). Place one drop on the sliding surfaces of the crossheads (the parts behind the pistons, that move back and forth). Do NOT lubricate any of the tender trucks or the trucks under freight or passenger cars; just pop out the wheels by spreading the truck side frames and clean the bearings and the tips of the axles thoroughly with contact cleaner or alcohol.

SOUND SYSTEMS FOR STEAM

LGB offers several European prototype diesels with sounds, ranging from a simple horn to a speed-synchronized diesel roar, with idle. A European 2080S prototype steam engine has been available with steam sound system. The latest American prototype, 2019S, includes whistle, bell, and chuff synchronized to speed.

For other locomotives, Starr Enterprises is one of several firms that sell a sound system that uses a battery for power. Such a system can be mounted in a modified mogul tender or inside a freight car. Starr and several other firms offer electronic sound systems that use the track to carry a signal so you can control the timing of the sound and hear a faint bell or whistle.

Keller's Onboard carrier/command-control system (see Chapter 9) is also available with sound. The complete system can be mounted inside the 2028D LGB Mogul tender. The Onboard sound is controlled from the same hand-held key pad that holds the throttle and reverse controls. You can vary the steam exhaust, air pump, whistle, and bell timing and tone by remote control from the key pad.

Other carrier/command-control systems can be used to power whistles driven with 12-volt blowers, treating them as though they were engine motors.

The Keller Onboard system of carrier/command-control utilizes this compact electronic unit fitted inside the tender of an LGB mogul. This unit has the optional sound unit that generates steam, air pump, whistle, and bell sounds to be played from the speaker in the tender but controlled by the Onboard key pad. Photo courtesy Keller Engineering.

One modeler cut down an inexpensive Lifelike whistle, removed from a kit called "Whistling Billboard" for use with HO trains, mounted it in a 3019 postal car which comes with an electrical pick-up, and wired it to the car lights through a locomotive receiver for the Zero One carrier/command control system. Pitch varies with the "speed" sent to that receiver by a properly coded system engine controller, making possible various mournful "Whoo, whooos."

Chapter 14
Other Ways To Play

Permanent indoor and outdoor layouts have been the focus of this book. But there are other ways to play with Lehmann's entrancing trains, including temporary layouts and supporting activities that increase the enjoyment of the usual uses.

TEMPORARY LAYOUTS: CHRISTMAS

The tradition of the Christmas train is widespread in America. The brightly colored LGB trains enliven a room when they run around the base of a Christmas tree. Joe and Shirley McClain decorate their Victorian house a month before Christmas day, devoting their sunroom to the Christmas tree. The LGB trains are on two bent loops, one elevated and partly overlapping the other, with a multitude of dollhouse figures and accessories from Shirley's collection placed around the layout.

Another delightful use of the Christmas train is delivering presents from a loop of track to family members seated around the tree. At Ann and Carter Colwell's house, a 2017D pulls a short train of green,

Al Kincaid, Brad Eggeman, and Norm Grant assembled these LGB layouts on indoor/outdoor carpeting for the Denver, Colorado Modelmania exposition in 1987.

red, and silver cars with the gift usually placed in an open 4020 gondola. For a heavy gift, such as a food processor, a four-axle 4062 car can be used.

TEMPORARY LAYOUTS: MODULES AND OTHER MODES

Since LGB track is both sturdy and sectional, it can be transported disassembled, and quickly rejoined to make a display. The late Al Lentz, founder of the LGB Big Train Operator's Club, took display loops to National Model Railroad Association conventions and set up shopping center displays for various charities where hopper cars stopped before prospective donors.

The phenomenal success of N-Trak, a standard for N Gauge *modules* and the special interest group that assembles their individual modules into massive show systems, has begun to influence modelers in other scales. The main requirement for compatibility is a standard height and at least one through track. A flat face at the ends of the modules helps join them securely. Most groups join modules with bolts through end-holes spaced to an agreed standard, but the simplest way to connect modules so that individual wobble won't distort the connecting track is to add two C-clamps per joint. A standard setback of the through track is not necessary, but gives the layout a more even front edge, desirable if many viewers pass by. Another desirable standard includes power inter-connections, providing each module's private pack with house current for accessories and internal train switching.

You can have your own individual system of modules, for easy transportation to group meetings and other showings, as modelers Skip Stundis and

---

Some guidelines for displays:

1. Keep fragile structures out of the flow of traffic.
2. Put your best work where it can be seen.
3. If you expect guests to circulate, provide clear indications of the usual flow of traffic with paths, railings, and signs.
4. Plan several independent operations. If one falters, the others will keep going.
5. For display of expensive and rare equipment to the public, for example in a shopping center, keep trains out of reach with a gap between railing and layout, or a safety glass or plastic shield along the front.
6. Be sure you understand the insurance situation before displaying in public areas. This can be a sensitive and potentially costly issue.

Russell Bitcon do. But most modular operation is a group activity. If there is a group in your area with modular standards, it makes sense to follow those standards.

DISPLAY LAYOUTS

A display layout is usually temporary and often portable; if it is large, modular construction helps. Railroaders who like the spectator role are in effect building themselves display layouts.

When you are planning a home layout, it is how visitors see it — that is, where they stand or sit to see the trains, where they can walk without tearing up your catenary, what features you want them to notice, and what the trains will do by themselves while you talk — that will all affect planning, particularly of indoor aisles and outdoor paths. Aisles, two feet wide, are adequate for one-way traffic, but should be at least three feet wide for cul-de-sacs where people will be entering and leaving simultaneously.

Remember, too, that your guests won't know what breaks and what doesn't. Let them know in advance where they are welcome and where they are not, with signs, railings, and other route markers.

Designing a small display layout can be fun. A simple passing siding, ending in two stubs, with the turnout at each end spring-loaded to route the engine up one track and down the other, can be used with reversing circuitry to keep a locomotive moving through two routes. If space permits, the two siding tracks don't have to be exactly parallel.

With an uncoupler in each track of the siding, a single car will follow a pattern different from the continuous run of the engine, as it is pushed into and pulled from one stub, left on the siding while the engine runs around it, and then pushed into and pulled from the other stub.

Up to three cars, or strings of cars, if your sidings are long enough and you deactivate all couplers from car to car within each string, can be switched on such a layout at a time. However, two is more interesting since the engine is not always pulling a car into the siding and pulling one out.

Note: This system doesn't work with Kadee couplers, which require a little jerk in the middle of the uncoupling action. With LGB hook-and-loop or knuckle-style couplers, you must experiment to determine whether coupling speed and uncoupling speed are the same. If they are not, an insulated section of track in the passing sidings must have its own speed regulator, to allow slowing for uncoupling.

Figure 14-1.

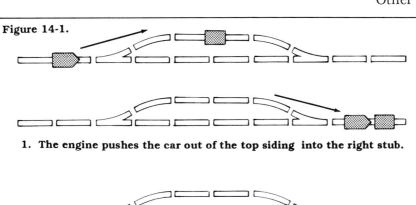

1. The engine pushes the car out of the top siding into the right stub.

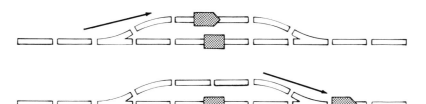

2. The engine pulls the car out of the right stub into the bottom siding, where it uncouples.

3. The engine runs around the car via the left stub, top siding, and the right stub.

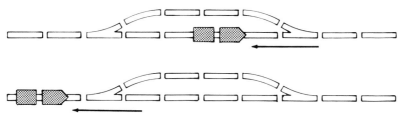

4. The engine pushes the car out of the bottom siding into the left stub.

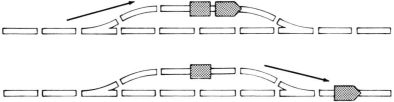

5. The engine pulls the car out of the left stub into the top siding, where it uncouples.

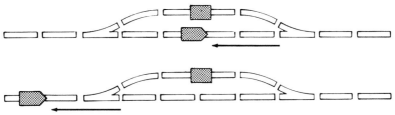

6. The engine runs around the car via the right stub, the bottom siding, and the left stub; and the cycle begins again at the top siding.

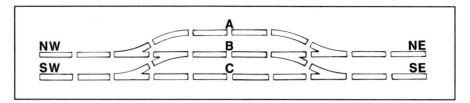

Locomotive X travels the route NW, A, NE, B, NW; locomotive Y travels the route SW, C, SE, B, SW. The engines alternate one-way trips, X waiting at NE stub for Y to reach SE stub, Y then waiting at SE stub for X to reach NW stub before itself returning to SW stub. The turnout from B to NW and SW must be powered; the rest can be spring-loaded.

A more complex version of this display, consisting of two passing sidings sharing one track, and a total of four stubs, with two engines running alternately, can shuffle up to five cars back and forth from one engine's route to the other's. Each engine, as it enters a stub, activates a 1700 track contact that throws a 1201 and 1203 *relay* that turns off its current and turns on the other engines. All turnouts but one can be spring-loaded. The exit turnout from the common track must be electrically directed, to steer each engine alternately into its own stub. Such a layout can be operated continuously without adjustment for up to eight hours. More commonly, speed needs to be reset at intervals of a few hours.

For a continuous route, bear in mind general principles of good layout design. Provide some kind of view interrupter such as a tunnel, buildings, or a scenic ridge that at least partially obscures some of the train as it goes by. These add interest and increase its apparent length.

An attractive mountain display in a fairly narrow space can be made with the 2046 electric rack locomotive. Several switchbacks, or stubs in the main line as in a zigzag, can reverse a short train back and forth as it climbs from one level to another. The turnouts must be level, both because there is no turnout available in the rack itself and because the grade is changing from one tilt to the other at each turnout. Reversing circuitry, either the more complex relays to install (such as 1201 plus 1203) or the easy to install 0090 automatic reversing unit, would automate operation.

But complication is not necessary. George Nachwalter's simple shelf display (see page 35) shows that with skillfully-made backgrounds, a straight back-and-forth run can be very attractive.

SUPPORTING THE FICTION

Part of the fun of running a train is to make believe that it is a real railroad. Not only does your train look like an actual railroad, but you can envision that it operates like one, too. This fiction can be maintained by peripheral activities that need not involve operating the actual layout.

Histories: Make up a history of your railroad. Decide what part of the country it serves and how it connects to other railroads; a stub running into a

A possible display rack railroad. Minimum length, with two-foot stubs so a car may be pulled, is two feet for each switch plus clearance for curves, three-foot 12 percent-average transitional grades at each switch, and two-foot 25 percent grades, (making a total of sixteen feet), the maximum rise is one foot each switchback, or two feet total rise. However, tests should be made to ensure that the vertical curves are not too abrupt. Use very short track sections, which can bend a little at the joint, to make the vertical curves. The practical minimum length may in fact be longer than sixteen feet.

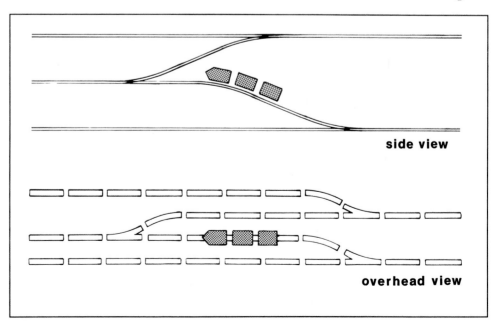

blind tunnel can represent interchange with other roads.

Consider what industries and companies provide its primary revenues and how they will receive raw materials, fuel, and empties, and send out finished products; why passengers use it (as commuters, tourists, shoppers, to attend special events or seasonal sports); how ownership and control have shifted, and how new management has altered equipment by repainting or purchase/sale; and how a few local legends (such as its infamous lovers' leap, great landslide, or the time Running Bear broke out of the reservation) figure into the railroad's history. If you have a specific locale for your road, some research into local history can give authenticity to your "imagineering."

Names: Pick your railroad's name carefully. Perhaps the most famous of HO layouts, John Allen's Gorre and Daphetid, gained mythic stature from his innovations in modeling techniques, his professional photography, and the fire that destroyed the layout two weeks after he died. The name, which he kept from his tiny table top layout through the final basement empire, is a pun to be pronounced "gory and defeated" — which presumably is how he expected to feel upon completing his layout. He commented once he should have chosen a less frivolous name, as the joke wore thin over the decades. Names such as "Thawtticood, Makitu, & Align," pronounced "Thought I could make it to end o' line," may pall sooner than you think in the thrill of the creative moment.

Family names will be more satisfactory over the long haul if they are disguised enough to sound like genuine place names. The K C C J & J, a short line from Knox City through Christopher Junction to Joshuaville, enshrines the names of three sons: Knox Cadman (called Casey), Christopher James, and Joshua. Other personalized name sources include initials, foreign or original forms of a name, and derivatives of a name's meaning; a dictionary of names gives the original meaning of both common and unusual names.

For a fictional history based on an actual geographic location, such as a feeder line between two

The logo on the Lehmann company stationery.

real railroads, it is a matter of choosing the right real towns as terminal points or as through-stops en route. For example, the Rhaetian Railroad in southeast Switzerland at one time planned an extension up the valley of the Inn, to cross into Austria and connect there. Your line might be an independent fulfillment of that intention, connecting with the end terminus of the Austrian Zillertalbahn, and named the Tarasp and Mayerhofen International, and run the equipment of both the Rhaetian and Zillertal that Lehmann has marketed. Or you could combine real names with a site created for the new railroad. Railroads named every stopping point in the belief that "Bellyful Gulch" is more memorable to train crews than "milepost 73.7."

When railroad author Charles S. Small named his backyard line, he chose a name that could account for the initials "LGB" (which appeared more prominently on the older equipment than nowadays): Lake George and Boulder. A ready-made logo for the Tarasp and Mayerhofen International is "TM" for trademark. You may wish to name your railroad with re-lettering, logos, and slogans in mind.

Paper Stuff: Once you have selected or designed a name, a logo, and/or a slogan, then you can have them imprinted onto stationery, passes (which can be passed out to new acquaintances like business cards), schedules, and route maps. The Lehmann company stationery, shown above, includes a full-sized 2020 steamer head-on, in a faint line drawing filling most of the page; their envelopes are printed with a color photo of the beginner's set, 20301, on the back. Color printing is costly, but most of us can afford black and white if the printer doesn't have to supply the artwork.

Glossary

Articulated: a type of steam locomotive equipped with two separate sets of driving wheels and cylinders. One set of drivers can pivot from side to side to allow the locomotive to negotiate sharper radius curves. Some are also called Mallets when the front set of cylinders is larger than the rear.

Ballast: the rocks or cinders used to fill the gaps between railroad ties and around track. Model railroads use crushed or small-sized gravel for ballast. Several commercial brands are available.

Birney: a type of trolley car.

Block: a section of track isolated electrically, with insulated rail joiners and separate wire connections to allow the operation of two or more trains on the same layout, or to prevent short circuits in a reverse loop.

Branch: a separate segment of track, usually from one to 100 miles long, leading to towns or industries away from the railroad's main line of operations.

Building flat: a building facade placed against the rear of layout (or backdrop) to give the impression that a whole building is present.

Carrier control: see Command Control.

Catenary system: wiring suspended above railway tracks to supply high voltage current for electric locomotives. On real or model electric locomotives, there is either a pantograph (a jointed device) or a straight trolley pole, mounted on the roof to collect current from the catenary wire.

Chuff: the spelling of a steam locomotive sound.

Command control: any of several systems (including Onboard, Dynatrol, Zero One, and some described in hobby magazine construction articles) of sending coded electrical control signals through the rails to engines equipped with decoders, so that several engines can be independently controlled in the same track circuit.

Common rail: a system of connecting the electrical wires to several blocks on the track that joins all the wires from one "common" rail to one terminal on the power pack to reduce the number of connections, insulated rail gaps, and wires.

Continuous running: operating a train around a circuit of track without interference.

Crossing: when two tracks cross or "X" each other on the same level.

Crossover: when two turnouts are used to connect two parallel tracks so a train can cross from one track to the other.

Cut: the notch or gap formed in a hill or mountain when a railroad right of way digs into it to maintain a level right of way.

Cyanoacrylate: fast-setting glue. Known as "super-glue."

Diode: an electrical device, consisting of a small cylinder on a wire, that allows current to flow in one direction only; many applications to track wiring, including reversing loops, stub sidings, and one-way stopping sections.

DPDT: stands for double pole, double throw — two independent inputs (double pole) can be connected to two independent outputs each (double throw). An electrical toggle or slide switch used to select two different blocks or to select either of two power packs for one block: a block selector. Can alternatively be wired to reverse the current or polarity and thus reverse the train: a reversing switch.

Duck-unders: a bridge section of a model railroad line that allows the modeler to "duck under" to reach an access pit or opening inside the layout table.

EAV: label for older LGB locomotives. They require more than normal voltage before they will operate. This feature allows them to sit still at a station while another locomotive conducts switching moves.

Facing point turnout: how a turnout faces relative to the direction the train is traveling. If a moving train can enter the diverging route without changing directions, it is a facing point turnout. See "trailing point turnout" and "runaround."

Fill: the piles of dirt the real railroads used to bring the bottom of a valley up to the prevailing grade of the right of way. A long, dam-like section of dirt positioned to support the tracks.

Flange: the sharp edges of any railroad car wheel or locomotive driver. That portion of the wheel that keeps the locomotive or car from sliding sideways off the track or rail.

Flex-track: flexible sections of model railroad track.

Gap: a break or cut in the rails with some type of electrical insulation to keep the break from closing accidentally. Gaps are used to isolate electrically some section of the track or rail to prevent short circuits or to allow the independent operation of two or more trains at once.

Gauge: the distance between the inside faces of the tops of the rails. The "standard" gauge for most full-sized American railroads is 4 feet 8-1/2 inches. See Narrow Gauge.

Grade: an up or down hill portion of the track. Grades are measured by their steepness; cited as a ratio (1 in 25; 4 in 100) or as a percentage (4 percent).

Grab-iron: the metal bars or rungs used by railroad men to hold onto the sides or ends of cars.

Ground foam: pulverized (finely-ground) styrofoam that is dyed for use as grass, earth, sand, etc. on train layouts. Also used in architectural modules.

Half-wave direct current: an electrical potential whose wave form is exactly half of an alternating current wave form. Also called "half-wave rectified alternating current."

Industry: short-hand term to describe cars used or owned by the major industries (corporations) served by them.

Interchange: the track that connects one real railroad with another. The place where the cars from one railroad are handed over to another railroad.

Interlocking: when a single switch or lever can be thrown to automatically set a route for the trains, including setting the track side signals that indicate open or closed routes.

Interurban: the real railroads that use electricity taken from overhead wires for power and that operate between two or more cities rather than just within a single city.

Jumper wire: a conductor wire used to make a temporary electrical connection or to connect two electrical blocks.

Lap siding: a track configuration that allows three trains to pass on a single-track main line. See Figure 5-6 in text.

L-girder: two pieces of wood butted together in an L-shape to be used for layout benchwork. A very sturdy construction technique.

Layout: a complete model railroad's track, scenery, and buildings.

Loop-to-loop: a track plan or system of operation wherein a train operates between two reversing loops (see entry), running back and forth on the main line connecting them and turning around in the loop at each end.

Make-up track: a small section of track used in track arrangements that do not balance with full sections.

Main line: the most-used and most direct tracks between major cities.

Mallet: a compound steam locomotive with two sets of drivers, such as an 0-6-6-0 or 2-8-8-2.

Module: a layout segment built to conform with a set of standards to allow the assembly of several units into a complete layout. Most often, modules are built by individuals and assembled at train shows or club gatherings.

Mogul: a steam engine with a 2-6-0 wheel arrangement.

Narrow gauge: describes both the track and the entire railroad when the track gauge is less than the standard 4 feet 8-1/2 inches. In the United States, the most common narrow gauge is 3 feet between the tops of the rails but there are also quite a few railroads, particularly in Maine, and at industrial sites that are 2 foot gauge. Meter gauge is the most common narrow gauge in Europe, the distance between the railheads being a meter or about 39 inches.

Open grid: type of wood construction placing boards at right angles, horizontally and vertically. A useful technique in building indoor layout tables.

Out-and-back: a track plan or system of operation wherein trains depart from a stub terminal and eventually reach a reversing loop (see entry), turn through it, and return to the stub terminal.

Passing siding: two parallel tracks that are connected at both ends with turnouts or switches so trains can enter or exit from either end of either track.

Point-to-point: a track plan or a system of operation regardless of track plan, that runs trains from one point to another and then back; not a circle or loop for continuous running.

Point-to-loop: see out-and-back.

Points: the portions of a turnout that actually move to change the train's route from the straight to the diverging track.

Power pack: the electrical device for connecting household current into model train current (for LGB, 110 volt AC to 18 volt DC); may or may not include a throttle.

Prototype: the real thing; the full-sized railroads that modelers and manufacturers of models attempt to duplicate in miniature.

Rail joiner: a bent piece of metal (or plastic, if it is an insulated rail joiner) used to join the ends of two rails or two track sections on a model railroad.

Reed switch: a magnetically-operated device for opening and closing electrical circuits.

Reefer: the enclosed cars that are fitted with insulation to help keep their loads cold. The narrow gauge reefers have bins or bunkers in each end that are filled, from floor to ceiling, with ice to keep the contents cool. Modern railroads use mechanical cooling systems that function much like a household refrigerator.

Relay: an electrical switch, for routing current, operated mechanically, by a switch-throwing device that is itself operated and controlled by electricity. Combining LGB's DPDT (1203) with LGB's turnout-control mechanism (1201) creates a relay, whether 1201 is attached to a turnout or not.

Reversing loop: a P-shaped track arrangement that forces any train entering the bottom of the P to turn around and exit the bottom of the P heading in the opposite direction. A handy track pattern to reverse the direction of entire trains.

Right of way: the railroad property that includes the rails, ties, ballast, drainage ditches beside the track, and at least enough clearance on either side for the largest locomotive to pass.

Runaround: a passing siding where a locomotive pulling a train can uncouple from the train to use the adjacent parallel track to move around to the rear so the locomotive can push the train, rather than pulling it. A move necessary in order to push a car into a facing point siding.

Sectional track: model railroad track that is preformed as far as curvature (if any) and length are concerned. LGB brand track is sectional.

Side tank: a water tank, usually in pairs, mounted on either side of a locomotive boiler.

Slave: an electrical device that is controlled by another electrical device (the "master").

Spot: to park a freight or passenger car on a siding; to place a car in a particular track location.

SPST: single pole, single throw on-off switch.

Standard gauge: on real railroads, the track gauge of 4 feet 8-1/2 inches. On model railroads, a track gauge first used in 1906 by Lionel of about 2-1/8 inches, close to that used by LGB (45 mm or 1-5/6 inches). Marklin still makes 1/32 scale models of West German equipment as accurate models. Aster and others make relatively expensive American-prototype metal models. Today, those accurate 1/32 scale models are sometimes called "Gauge 1" to differentiate them from LGB equipment.

Stopping section: a section of track wired (often with a diode; perhaps by power routing through turnout relays) so that a locomotive entering it automatically comes to a stop.

Stub siding: siding that dead ends at a certain point.

Switch: technically, only an electrical device to route power like an on-off or a reversing switch or a light switch. Some modelers refer to the tracks that allow the trains a choice of two or more diverging routes as switches, but *turnout* is a more appropriate term.

Switch back: a track configuration used mostly in mountainous areas to allow a train to ascend a grade in a small space.

Switching: the act of moving a car with a locomotive, such as placing a boxcar on a siding.

Template: a plastic or metal plate that is pre-cut for special shapes, such as track switches, electrical controls, etc., so that they may be traced onto a plan.

Tender: the car that is pulled behind a steam locomotive to carry fuel and water for that locomotive. Some steam locomotives have water tanks on each side of the boiler and a fuel bunker behind the cab; they do not need a tender. Those engines are usually called "tank" engines.

Throttle: the speed control for the locomotive. On a live-steam locomotive, the device controlling the opening that lets the steam into the engine's cylinders. In model railroading, the speed and direction controls (commonly a rheostat adding resistance or a potentiometer regulating voltage through transistors, plus a DPDT reversing switch). See "Power Pack."

Tie-strip: flexible pieces of plastic used to connect curved pieces of track or to extend straight track sections.

Trailing point turnout: how a turnout faces relative to the direction the train is traveling. If a moving train must back up or reverse to enter the diverging route, it is a trailing point turnout for that direction of travel. See "Facing point turnout." The difference matters when switching cars; see "Runaround."

Trolley: the electric "buses" that run on rails and collect their electric operating current from overhead wires. Generally, trolleys operate in towns and are not much larger than buses, while interurbans have a similar appearance but are larger cars.

Truck: the device that holds the two (or more) wheels and axles under each end of a freight car, passenger car, locomotive, or tender. The truck pivots to allow the vehicle to negotiate a tighter curve without derailing.

Turning section: a section of model track where a locomotive rejoins its previous route, but is facing in the opposite direction; part of a reversing loop or a wye, or a turntable. The turning section must be insulated at both ends and receive its power through special wiring, to prevent short circuits.

Turnout: the track that allows trains to travel from a single track into one or more diverging tracks. See "switch."

Turntable: a rotating bridge that is used to turn a locomotive end-for-end in the least amount of space.

Web/base of rail:

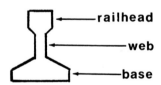

Well tank: a water tank slung between the locomotive wheels (or the engine that has one, such as the 2010D).

Wye: a space-consuming track configuration that enables the turning of whole trains, if the "tail" track is long enough. At a branch line terminal, the tail might be just long enough for the engine and one car. If located where another route already diverges at a sharp angle, the wye consumes little extra space, and can be installed at the economical cost of just one more switch. On the layout, where wye operation is fascinating to watch, a special insulated section of track, with reversible current polarity, is necessary to avoid a short circuit. (See illustration on page 81.)

Appendix

CLUBS

See "Publications" below

LGB Model Railroad Club
Gail Nagie, Secretary-Treasurer
P. O. Box 7282
Baden, Pennsylvania 15005
(412) 375-8286

- Big Train Operator *magazine, quarterly, with $16 annual membership*

National Model Railroaders' Association (NMRA)
4121 Cromwell Road
Chattanooga, Tennessee 37421

- *Monthly NMRA Bulletin (N6633 Waukesha Avenue, Sussex, Wisconsin 53089, (414) 246-4577); $22 membership dues includes subscription.*

NTrak
Jim Fitzgerald
2424 Alturas Road
Atascadero, California 93422
(805) 466-1758

- *Bimonthly newsletter; $8/year. Although strictly N scale, their standards for modular interchange may be of interest to LGB groups.*

Toy Train Operators' Society (TTOS)
25 West Walnut Street
Suite 408
Pasadena, California 91103
(818) 578-0673

- *Bimonthly* Bulletin *and bimonthly* Order Board; *one-time $15 initiation fee and $22 yearly dues*

PUBLICATIONS

Big Train Operators

- *40-page newsletter, b & w illus., with membership in LGB Club; see "Clubs" above*

Garden Railways
P. O. Box 61461
Denver, Colorado 80206

- *$18 per year (six issues)/$24 for foreign subscribers; exclusively outdoor model railroading; Marc Horovitz, editor*

The Gauge One Journal
P. O. Box 121
Cheltenham, Pennsylvania 19012

- *Send SASE for prices; mostly 1/32 scale, little 1/24, some LGB; Bill McIntyre, editor*

Kalmbach Publishing Company
see *Model Railroader*

- *many books on model railroading, some relevant to LGB*

LGB-Depesche
Ernst Paul Lehmann Patentwerk
Saganer Strasse 1-5
D-8500 Nuremberg 50
West Germany

- *$16 per year (3 issues) (price depends on exchange rate), published by Lehmann in German only. Prototype and model photos, some in color; layout descriptions; a few construction articles*

Model Railroader
1027 North Seventh Street
Milwaukee, Wisconsin 53233-1471

- *$27.95 per year (12 issues); largest-selling model magazine; Russell G. Larson, editor*

Model Railroading
2901 Blake Street
Denver, Colorado 80205

- *$28 per year (12 issues); prototype articles plus N, HO, O, and some LGB*

Narrow Gauge and Short Line Gazette
P. O. Box 26
Los Altos, California 94023

- *$18 per year (six issues); prototype and models fine scale; Bob Brown, editor*

Railroad Model Craftsman
Box 700
Newton, New Jersey 07860

- *$23 per year (12 issues); mostly HO, N, and O with some prototypes; William Schaumberg, editor*

SUPPLY SOURCES

There are several thousand hobby shops in this country, but only about a fourth of them actually carry LGB equipment and the accessory items in this scale from other firms. Many of the items in this book are available to any dealer willing to order them for you, either from the manufacturer or from one of the larger wholesale distributors like Walthers. Walthers publishes an extensive catalogue, but most of the items of interest to you will be tools, paints, and books.

To find hobby shops in your area or in any city or town you might visit, look in the telephone book's Yellow Pages under the heading "Hobby & Model Construction Supplies — Retail." You may also want to see some of the house kits, windows, and accessories for 1/2 inch-to-the-foot dollhouses and miniatures. Those dealers are listed under either "Dollhouses & Accessories" or "Miniatures for Collectors."

The firms listed below usually have catalogues and most of them charge for those catalogues at prices that can vary from $ .50 to $15 or more. If you write to any of these firms, enclose a stamped, self-addressed envelope (SSAE) if you expect any kind of reply. Many of these firms are very small or part-time businesses and their owners have neither the time nor the profit margin to engage in lengthy correspondence with potential customers. It is common courtesy to include an SSAE with any inquiry. They also like to know where customers have read about their products.

AMSI Model Supplies
P. O. Box 750638
Petaluma, California 94975

- *trees, bushes, and foam for indoors*

Aristo-Craft: see Polks

Back Woods Car Shop
Route 3, Box 518A
DeSoto, Missouri 63020

- *wood and metal freight car kits; dry transfers*

CDS Lettering Ltd.
P. O. Box 2003, Station D
Ottawa, Ontario K1P 5W3, Canada

- *dry transfer lettering; $6 for catalogue*

Charles Ro Supply Company
347A Pleasant Street
Malden, Massachusetts 02148

- *billboard freight cars, work train*

Chuck's Custom Cars
14918 Lake Forest
Dallas, Texas 75240

- *limited production built-up freight cars*

Champion Decal Company
P. O. Box 1178
Minot, North Dakota 58702

- *Champ O scale decals*

Dallee Electronics
Box 1921
Reading, Pennsylvania 19603

- *power packs, throttles, and electronics*

Delton Locomotive Works
120 Maple
Delton, Michigan 49046

- *ready-to-run cars and locomotives, couplers*

Depot G Hobbies
OS 371 Florida Lane
Winfield, Illinois 60190

- *structure kits*

Robert Dustin
334 Auburndale Avenue
Newton, Massachusetts 02166

- *decals for cars and locomotives; $6 for catalogue*

Dynatrol Command Control: see Power Systems, Inc.

Ertl Company
Highways 136 & 20
Dyersville, Iowa 52040

- *Ertl and MPC plastic kits and metal vehicles*

Evergreen Scale Models
1414 127th Place, N.E., Suite 107
Bellevue, Washington 98005

- *styrene plastic sheets and strips*

Garden Railway Company
2009 Madison Road
Cincinnati, Ohio 45208

- *custom builds and designs outdoor layouts*

Floquil-Polly S Color Corporation
Route 30 North
Amsterdam, New York 12010

- *Floquil paints, Polly S acrylics and brushes*

Gargraves Trackage Corporation
RD 1, Box 255A
South Rose, New York 14516

- *ready-to-lay and kit track and turnouts*

Carl Goldberg Models, Inc.
4732 West Chicago Avenue
Chicago, Illinois 60651

- *super glues including Super Jet and Super T*

Grant Line Products
1040-B Shary Court
Concord, California 94518

- *plastic windows and detail parts*

Heki: *trees, foam, and flocking available to dealers through:*
Portman Hobby Distributors
851 Washington Street
Peeksill, New York 10566

Hot Stuff/Satellite City
P. O. Box 836
Simi, California 93065

- *super glues including Super T*

Industrial Miniatures
Route 1, Box 169B
Milbank, South Dakota 57252

- *built-up structures*

Kadee Quality Products
720 South Grape Street
Medford, Oregon 97501

- *couplers and ramps*

Kalamazoo Toy Train Works
541 Railroad Street
Bangor, Michigan 49013

- *ready-to-run cars, locomotives, and track*

Keller Engineering
200 San Mateo Avenue
Los Gatos, California 95030

- *ONBOARD carrier/command-control systems*

Kenosha Railway Supply Ltd.
P. O. Box 39096
Denver, Colorado 80239

- *custom-built wood bridges and kits*

Korber Scale Models
P. O. Box 101
Clementon, New Jersey 08021

- *plastic building kits*

L & P Trackworks
1345 Via Christina
Vista, California 92084

- *signs, barrels, and detail parts*

LaBelle oils: *distributed by*
JMC International
P. O. Box 328
Bensenville, Illinois 60106

The Laredo Line
P. O. Box 9006
Dallas, Texas 75209

- *custom-made building kits*

Life-Like Products, Inc.
1600 Union Avenue
Baltimore, Maryland 21211

- *trees, foam, signals, and accessories*

Larry Lindsay
1004 South Washington
Denver, Colorado 80209

- *rail-bending tools and switch stand*

Lionel Trains
26750 Twenty-Three Mile Road
Mount Clemens, Michigan 48043

- *ready-to-run locomotives, cars, and track*

Miniature Plant Kingdom
4125 Harrison Grade Road
Sebastapol, California 95472

- *living potted plant starters, 30-page catalogue (not illus.), $2.50*

MRC/Model Rectifier Corporation
2500 Woodbridge Avenue
Edison, New Jersey 08817

- *power packs*

Model Die Casting, Inc. (MDC)
P. O. Box 926
Hawthorne, California 90250

- *freight car kits*

Model-Power
180 Smith Street
Farmingdale, New York 11735

- *lighting accessories*

New England Hobby Supply
71 Hillard Street
Manchester, Connecticut 06040

- *wood structure kits and accessories*

Northeast Narrow Gauge
P. O. Box 191
Wiscasset, Maine 04578

- *wood and metal locomotive and car kits*

Northeastern Scale Models
P. O. Box 727
Methuen, Massachusetts 01844

- *milled basswood strips and sheets*

North West Short Line
Box 423
Seattle, Washington 98111-0423

- *self-powered trucks and scale wheel sets*

Onboard Command Control: see Keller Engineering

Ozark Miniatures
P. O. Box 248
De Soto, Missouri 63020

- *detail castings*

Pola building kits: see Walthers

Polks Hobby International
346 Bergen Avenue
Jersey City, New Jersey 07304

- *Aristo power packs and accessories*

Power Systems Inc. (PSI)
56 Bellis Circle
Cambridge, Massachusetts 02140

- *Dynatrol Carrier/command-control systems*

Precision Scale Company
P. O. Box 1262
1120-A Gum Avenue
Woodland, California 95695

- *cast brass detail parts and ready-built cars, tank cars, and detail parts*

Preiser: see Walthers

- *scale model people and animals*

REA (Railway Express Agency, Inc.)
P. O. Box 1247
Milwaukee, Wisconsin 53201

- *locomotives, cars, and track*

Rail Britannia
P. O. Box 106
Whittier, California 90608

- *freight car conversion kits*

Rail Craft Products
1120 Eagle Road
Fenton, Missouri 63026

- *rail, spikes, and rail bending tools*

Rheinberger LGB Grossbahn-Center:
see Schaefer LGB Grossbahn-Center

Ro, Charles: see Charles Ro Supply Company

Schaefer LGB Grossbahn-Center
Ferdinandstrasse 30
D-6830 Bad Homburg V. D. H.
West Germany
Tel. 0 61 72/2 1373

- *locomotives, post-factory car modifications, European prototypes; flyer with colored illustrations. They ship to the United States*

Small Sales Company
P. O. Box 7803
Boise, Idaho 83707

- *1/2 inch-to-the-foot dollhouse windows and kits*

Short Line Foundry
412 Oak Glen
Plano, Texas 75074

- *cast detail parts*

Starr/Tri-Tec
P. O. Box 170
Deerfield, Illinois 60015

- *power packs and sound systems*

Tempest Electronics
P. O. Box 265
Ferntree Gully, Victoria 3156, Australia

- *radio control throttles*

Trackside Details
1331 Avalon Street
San Luis Obispo, California 93401

- *cast metal detail parts*

Two Points Five Models (John Row)
P. O. Box 187
Buffalo Creek, Colorado 80425

- *track cleaning devices and rail connectors*

Vintage Reproductions
P. O. Box 7098
Colorado Springs, Colorado 80933

- *flocking for scenery and dry transfer signs*

Wm. K. Walthers, Inc.
5601 West Florist Avenue
Milwaukee, Wisconsin 53218

- *distributors of Preiser, Somerfelt, Momod, and others*

C. L. Welch
316 Modesto Drive
San Bernardino, California 92404

- *cast resin tunnel portals*

Woodland Scenics
P. O. Box 98
Linn Creek, Missouri 65052

- *ground foam and tree kits*